JAN 1 3 2012

Inspired by the Elm Creek Quilts *Novels*

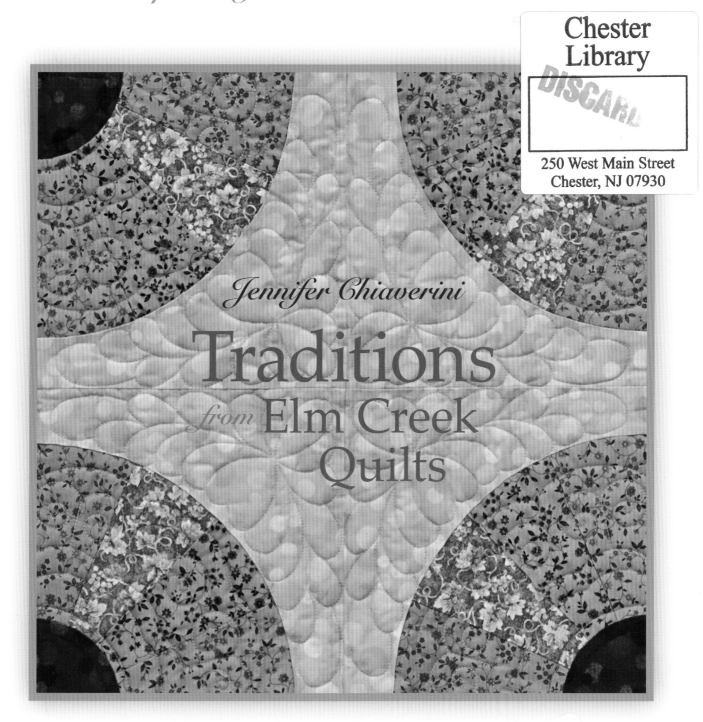

Jennifer Chiaverini

Traditions
from Elm Creek
Quilts

13 Quilt Projects to Piece & Appli~

D1288479

C&T PUBLISHING

Text and artwork copyright © 2011 by Jennifer Chiaverini

Photography copyright © 2011 by C&T Publishing, Inc.

Publisher: *Amy Marson*

Creative Director: *Gailen Runge*

Acquisitions Editor: *Susanne Woods*

Editor: *Deb Rowden*

Technical Editors: *Carolyn Aune and Gailen Runge*

Cover Designer: *Kristy Zacharias*

Book Designer: *Rose Sheifer-Wright*

Production Coordinator: *Jenny Leicester*

Production Editors: *Julia Cianci and S. Michele Fry*

Illustrator: *Jennifer Chiaverini*

Photography by *Christina Carty-Francis and Diane Pedersen*
of C&T Publishing, Inc., unless otherwise noted

Published by C&T Publishing, Inc., P.O. Box 1456, Lafayette, CA 94549

Dedication

To my mother, Geraldine Neidenbach; my sister, Heather Neidenbach; and my friend Sue Vollbrecht, who generously lent their talents to the creation of this book.

Library of Congress Cataloging-in-Publication Data

Chiaverini, Jennifer.

Traditions from Elm Creek quilts : 13 quilt projects to piece & appliqué / Jennifer Chiaverini.

   p. cm.

ISBN 978-1-60705-402-3 (soft cover)

1. Patchwork--Patterns. 2. Quilting--Patterns. 3. Patchwork quilts. I. Title.

TT835.C4595 2011

746.46'041--dc22

2011005878

Printed in China

10 9 8 7 6 5 4 3 2 1

Contents

Elm Creek Quilts
INSPIRATIONS

When I travel around the country on book tours, readers often ask me, "Where do you get your ideas?" Sometimes my fascination with a particular quilting style or a historical era inspires a new novel, but often a character, story line, or unanswered question from a previous book provides the seed that grows into a new novel.

The idea for *The Winding Ways Quilt*, my twelfth Elm Creek Quilts novel, came to me while I was writing the ninth book in the series. In *Circle of Quilters*, I introduced five new characters who were vying for two open positions on the faculty of Elm Creek Quilt Camp. As I told each new character's story, describing how each applicant had learned to quilt and developed an enduring love and respect for the art form, it occurred to me that I had not provided a similar artistic history for many of the characters that had been a part of the series from the beginning. I was sure that my longtime readers would be curious about how their favorite Elm Creek Quilters had become quilters, what had attracted them to the traditional art form, what patterns first appealed to them, who their first teachers were, and how they fared in their earliest attempts. By delving into each Elm Creek Quilter's past, I explored the unexpected twists and turns their lives had followed and how their choices had led them to Elm Creek Manor—and where their winding ways might take them next.

The book that followed, *The Quilter's Kitchen*, was also inspired by earlier stories—or, more accurately, by readers whose taste buds were inspired by earlier stories. Whenever my characters prepare a particularly tasty dish, readers contact me through my website or at book tour events to request the recipe. I've received hundreds of requests for the recipe for Gerda's apple strudel from *The Christmas Quilt* alone! Since I like to keep my readers happy, I thought it would be fun to select favorite dishes from the series, mix them together with a story, and serve them up for Elm Creek Readers to enjoy. With the exception of the anise-flavored spring bread, a recipe handed down from my husband's grandmother, Giuditta Chiaverini, all the recipes included in *The Quilter's Kitchen* were created by the renowned food writer Sally Sampson. Many of the original recipes Sally devised for *The Quilter's Kitchen* have become favorites in the Chiaverini home.

The heroine of my fourteenth novel, *The Lost Quilter*, is a runaway slave who first appeared in the fourth book in the series. When I wrote *The Runaway Quilt*, I deliberately didn't envision Joanna's life after her recapture and forced return to slavery in the South because I wanted her fate to remain a mystery to me, as it was to those who sheltered her at Elm Creek Farm—and to Sylvia, who discovered her story more than a century later in the pages of Gerda Bergstrom's memoirs. Joanna lingered in my imagination for years after *The Runaway Quilt* was published, however, and I often found myself puzzling over the many different paths her life might have taken. Eventually I decided to continue Joanna's story and find answers to some of the questions that remained after the close of *The Runaway Quilt*, especially why Joanna never returned to the Elm Creek Valley.

In *A Quilter's Holiday*, I returned to the present day to develop a theme I introduced in *The Quilter's Kitchen*. In the earlier story, master quilter Sylvia Bergstrom Compson Cooper and Anna Del Maso, the new head chef of Elm Creek Quilt

Whether they sew to welcome newborns or to raise funds for worthy causes, the quilters of the Elm Creek Valley, past and present, always use their talents to make their world a warmer, more comforting, more beautiful place.

Camp, are preparing the manor's kitchen for renovations after quilt camp has closed for the season. As Sylvia and Anna clear out cupboards, they discover cherished Bergstrom family heirlooms, including the woven cornucopia that served as the Bergstrom family's centerpiece on Thanksgiving. Each family member would place something into it that represented what he or she was especially thankful for that year. In *A Quilter's Holiday*, Sylvia revives this cherished family tradition with her friends by asking them to piece quilt blocks as symbols of their gratitude. As each quilter explains the meaning of her chosen quilt block, the reader discovers that character's uncertainties and conflicts as well as her hopes for the holiday season to come.

Elm Creek Quilter Bonnie Markham missed the revival of this Bergstrom family tradition, however, because my sixteenth novel, *The Aloha Quilt*, takes her across the ocean to the warm sunshine and tropical breezes of Hawaii. I had long been fascinated by the beauty and spiritual significance of the quilts Hawaii is best known for—the distinctive, intricate, large-scale, two-color appliqué designs inspired by the natural wonders and rich cultural traditions of the islands. Writing *The Aloha Quilt* allowed me to explore the traditions and artistry of Hawaiian quilting while giving reader favorite Bonnie an adventure all her own.

I returned to Pennsylvania in *The Union Quilters*, my seventeenth book, which was inspired by the Civil War research I conducted while writing *The Runaway Quilt*, *The Sugar Camp Quilt*, and *The Lost Quilter*. Within their pages I had explored antebellum Pennsylvania and Civil War–era South Carolina, but except for a few details mentioned in Gerda's memoirs, I had never described what befell the residents of the Elm Creek Valley during the Civil War. Life on the Northern home front—especially women's roles in that time and place—has not often been examined in historical fiction, and I am pleased that *The Union Quilters* brought attention to a neglected topic.

In my eighteenth novel, *The Wedding Quilt*, I did something that I imagine caught my readers by surprise: Rather than delve into the past, I leapt forward 25 years into the future, to the wedding day of one of Sarah and Matt McClure's twins. This perspective allowed me to recount important events in the Elm Creek Quilters' lives as they experienced them, while enriching the story by giving the characters time to reflect upon their greatest joys and deepest regrets.

While the source of inspiration for my Elm Creek Quilts novels varies from book to book, every story inspires me to create the lovely quilts my characters make. Whether they sew to welcome newborns or to raise funds for worthy causes, the quilters of the Elm Creek Valley, past and present, always use their talents to make their world a warmer, more comforting, more beautiful place. I hope that when you try your hand at the new patterns I offer you within the pages of this book, you'll find that you've done the same in your own corner of the world.

FROM
The Winding Ways Quilt

As *The Winding Ways Quilt* begins, the founding Elm Creek Quilters have hired a new chef as well as two new teachers to replace those who have decided to pursue other careers. As the newcomers arrive, they try to find their places within the close-knit group even as the original members confront their impending separation. At the same time, the women are also dealing with unexpected crises in their own personal lives—divorce, pregnancy, and dreams unrealized. Fortunately, they remember the lessons of the past and turn to one another for love and support instead of struggling alone.

As friends depart and newcomers try to find their places within the circle of quilters, Sylvia sews a tribute to the original Elm Creek Quilters, capturing the spirit of their friendship at the moment of its transformation. The traditional quilt pattern she chooses, Winding Ways, creates a mosaic of overlapping circles and intertwining curves, the curved pieces symbolic of a journey. In the novel, Sylvia's quilt is comprised of nine separate panels, which, when hung side by side, appear to be a unified whole. For the version offered here, I made one quilt but created the illusion of separate panels through careful fabric selection and placement.

Diane, another founding Elm Creek Quilter, is compelled to learn to quilt after visiting a local guild's show and discovering a Viewer's Choice ribbon on a quilt made by her next-door neighbor and fiercest rival. *Springtime in Waterford* uses the Providence block and bright colors evocative of a lovely Pennsylvania spring in full bloom.

The Winding Ways Quilt also recounts how several of the Elm Creek Quilters first met on one momentous day while browsing through Bonnie's quilt shop, Grandma's Attic. Judy, nine months pregnant, goes into labor while searching for the perfect border fabric for a crib quilt, which she wanted very much to complete before her baby's arrival. In the rush to the hospital, Judy leaves the unfinished quilt top behind. Eager to help, Bonnie, Summer, Gwen, Diane, and Agnes decide to finish the quilt—*Welcome, Baby Emily!*—in time for the mother and daughter's homecoming.

When [the] sections of the quilt were at last properly aligned on the wall, the Elm Creek Quilters stepped back to take in the display. An electric murmur passed through them as they admired the mosaic of overlapping circles and intertwining curves, the careful balance of dark and light hues, the unexpected harmony of the disparate fabrics and colors. Together the separate quilts created a wondrous design, many winding paths meeting, intersecting, parting; concentric circles like ripples from a stone cast into a pond, overlapping, including, uniting. Sylvia had ingeniously quilted the different sections so that the meticulous stitches seemed to flow from one section into the next, drawing them together, creating the illusion that they comprised a single quilt. Gazing upon Sylvia's creation, each woman could now see that her individual section was beautiful in and of itself—but was also part of a larger, more magnificent whole, a single quilt harmonizing their differences, embracing all that made each of them uniquely themselves…

"The Winding Ways quilt will remind us of friends who have left our circle to journey far away." Slipping the hanging rod from the sleeve, Sylvia removed Summer's portion from the wall and returned it to her. "When one of our circle must leave us, she'll take her section of the quilt with her as a reminder of the loving friends awaiting her return. The empty places on the wall will remind those of us left behind that the beauty of our friendship endures, even if great distances separate us. When the absent friend returns to Elm Creek Manor, she will hang her quilt in its proper space, and the loveliness of the whole will be restored."

Excerpted from *The Winding Ways Quilt*
by Jennifer Chiaverini

Winding Ways

From *The Winding Ways Quilt* by Jennifer Chiaverini

Designed and pieced by Jennifer Chiaverini, machine quilted by Sue Vollbrecht, 2009.

Finished Block: 6″ × 6″
Finished Quilt: 70″ × 70″
Number of Blocks: 81 Winding Ways blocks

Materials

Assorted dark fabrics for blocks: Approximately 4 yards total

Assorted light fabrics for blocks: Approximately 4 yards total

Medium green fabric for inner border: ⅝ yard

Dark floral fabric for outer border and binding: 2 yards (includes ⅝ yard for the binding)

Backing: 4⅜ yards

Batting: 78" × 78"

Cutting Instructions

Copy template patterns A, B, and C on page 9 onto template material.

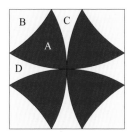

Dark block

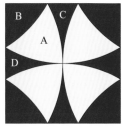

Light block

From Assorted Dark Fabrics

- Cut 164 A pieces.
- Cut 160 B pieces.
- Cut 80 C pieces.
- Cut 40 rectangles 2½" × 6½". Fold each rectangle in half and crease. Align the sewing line, not the seam allowance line, of the narrow end of template C along the fold. Trace around the template and cut out a D

shape, keeping the fabric folded and cutting through both layers. Unfold. Do not press; the crease will mark the center for ease of piecing later. Cut 40 D pieces.

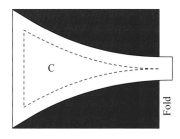

From Assorted Light Fabrics

- Cut 160 A pieces.
- Cut 164 B pieces.
- Cut 82 C pieces.
- Cut 41 rectangles 2½" × 6½". Fold each rectangle in half, crease, and cut as indicated above for the dark D pieces. Cut 41 D pieces.

From Medium Green Fabric

Cut 6 strips 2½" × width of fabric (for the inner border).

From Dark Floral Fabric

Cut 7 strips 6½" × width of fabric (for the outer border).

Block Assembly

1. To make the dark blocks, sew each dark A to a light B, matching the centers. Press toward the dark fabric. Make 164.

2. Sew 2 A/B units to opposite sides of each light C. Press toward the dark fabric. Make 82.

3. Sew 1 light D piece to an A/B/C row created in the previous step, using the crease to center the piece on the row. Press. Make 41.

4. Sew another A/B/C row to the remaining side of the D piece, centering the crease as before. Press. Make 41 dark blocks.

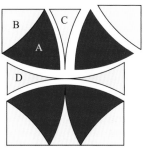

Make 41.

5. To make the light blocks, sew each light A to a dark B, matching the centers. Press toward the dark fabric. Make 160.

6. Sew 2 A/B units to opposite sides of each dark C. Press toward the dark fabric. Make 80.

7. Sew 1 dark D piece to an A/B/C row created in the previous step, using the crease to center the piece on the row. Press. Repeat to make 40.

8. Sew another A/B/C row to the remaining side of the D piece, centering the crease as before. Press. Make 40 light blocks.

Make 40.

Quilt Construction

1. Referring to the quilt photo on page 7, arrange the dark and light blocks, placing the similar fabrics together into nine-patch groups of 9 blocks each. Each group will contain either 4 lights with 5 darks or 5 lights with 4 darks. Make 9 of the nine-patch groups.

2. Stitch together each nine-patch group, sewing 3 rows of 3 blocks each. Press.

3. Sew the nine-patch groups together, sewing 3 rows of 3 groups each. Press.

4. Cut an inner border strip in half. Sew a half-strip to each of 2 long inner border strips and trim to make 2 borders 2½" × 54½". Sew to the sides of the quilt. Press toward the inner border.

5. Cut another inner border strip in half. Sew a half-strip to each of 2 long inner border strips and trim to make 2 borders 2½" × 58½". Sew to the top and bottom of the quilt. Press toward the inner border.

6. Cut an outer border strip in half. Sew a half-strip to each of 2 long outer border strips and trim to make 2 borders 6½" × 58½". Sew to the sides of the quilt. Press toward the outer border.

7. Sew the remaining outer border strips together in pairs end to end and trim to make 2 borders 6½" × 70½". Sew to the top and bottom of the quilt. Press toward the outer border.

8. Layer the quilt top, batting, and backing. Baste. Quilt as desired. Attach a hanging sleeve, if desired, and bind with the dark floral fabric.

Quilt Assembly Diagram

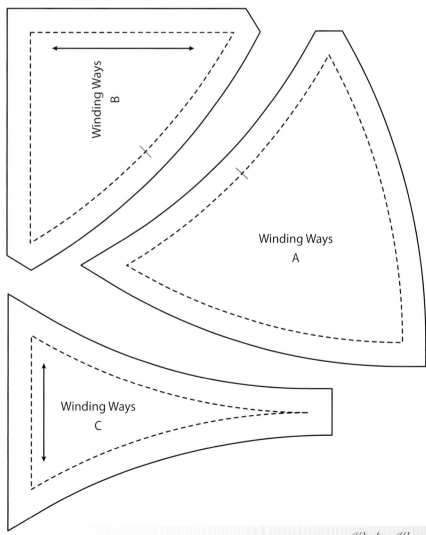

Winding Ways B

Winding Ways A

Winding Ways C

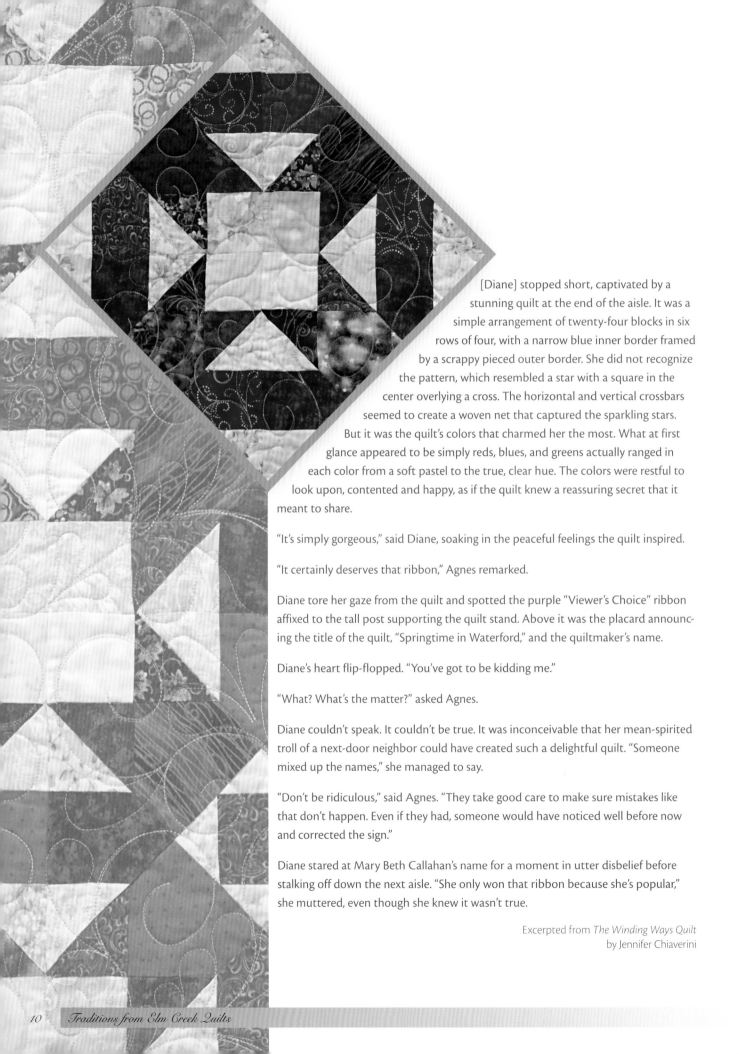

[Diane] stopped short, captivated by a stunning quilt at the end of the aisle. It was a simple arrangement of twenty-four blocks in six rows of four, with a narrow blue inner border framed by a scrappy pieced outer border. She did not recognize the pattern, which resembled a star with a square in the center overlying a cross. The horizontal and vertical crossbars seemed to create a woven net that captured the sparkling stars. But it was the quilt's colors that charmed her the most. What at first glance appeared to be simply reds, blues, and greens actually ranged in each color from a soft pastel to the true, clear hue. The colors were restful to look upon, contented and happy, as if the quilt knew a reassuring secret that it meant to share.

"It's simply gorgeous," said Diane, soaking in the peaceful feelings the quilt inspired.

"It certainly deserves that ribbon," Agnes remarked.

Diane tore her gaze from the quilt and spotted the purple "Viewer's Choice" ribbon affixed to the tall post supporting the quilt stand. Above it was the placard announcing the title of the quilt, "Springtime in Waterford," and the quiltmaker's name.

Diane's heart flip-flopped. "You've got to be kidding me."

"What? What's the matter?" asked Agnes.

Diane couldn't speak. It couldn't be true. It was inconceivable that her mean-spirited troll of a next-door neighbor could have created such a delightful quilt. "Someone mixed up the names," she managed to say.

"Don't be ridiculous," said Agnes. "They take good care to make sure mistakes like that don't happen. Even if they had, someone would have noticed well before now and corrected the sign."

Diane stared at Mary Beth Callahan's name for a moment in utter disbelief before stalking off down the next aisle. "She only won that ribbon because she's popular," she muttered, even though she knew it wasn't true.

Excerpted from *The Winding Ways Quilt*
by Jennifer Chiaverini

Springtime in Waterford

From *The Winding Ways Quilt* by Jennifer Chiaverini

Designed and pieced by Jennifer Chiaverini, machine quilted by Sue Vollbrecht, 2009.

Finished Block: 10″ × 10″

Finished Quilt: 48″ × 68″

Number of Blocks: 24 Providence blocks

Materials

Assorted red fabrics for blocks: ¾ yard total

Assorted blue fabrics for blocks and outer border: 1½ yards total

Assorted green fabrics for blocks: 1 yard total

Assorted cream fabrics for blocks, borders, and binding: 2⅞ yards (includes ½ yard each for the inner border and binding)

Backing: 3¼ yards

Batting: 56″ × 76″

Cutting Instructions

Copy template patterns A and B on page 13 onto template material.

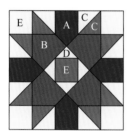

From Assorted Red Fabrics

● Cut 96 A pieces.

From Assorted Blue Fabrics

● Cut 96 B pieces.

● Cut 54 squares 2⅞″ × 2⅞″ (for the outer border).

From Assorted Green Fabrics

● Cut 96 squares 2⅞″ × 2⅞″. Cut each square in half diagonally once to make 192 C triangles.

● Cut 24 squares 2½″ × 2½″ (E).

From Assorted Cream Fabrics

● Cut 96 squares 2½″ × 2½″ (E).

● Cut 96 squares 2⅞″ × 2⅞″. Cut each square in half diagonally once to make 192 C triangles.

● Cut 24 squares 3¼″ × 3¼″. Cut each square in half diagonally twice to make 96 D triangles.

● Cut 54 squares 2⅞″ × 2⅞″ and 4 squares 2½″ × 2½″ (for the outer border).

● Cut 6 strips 2½″ × width of fabric (for the inner border).

Block Assembly

1. Sew 4 cream D triangles to each green E square. Press. Make 24.

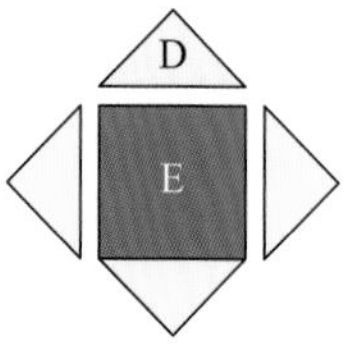

2. Sew 2 cream C triangles to opposite sides of each red A piece. Press. Make 96.

3. Sew 1 green C triangle to each cream E square. Press. Sew 1 green C triangle to each blue B piece. Press. Sew each C/E unit to a C/B unit. Press. Make 96.

4. Sew 2 units from Step 3 to opposite sides of a unit made in Step 1 to make a center diagonal row. Press. Make 24.

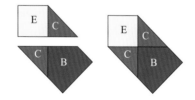

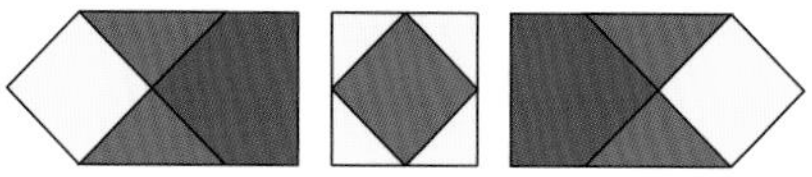

5. Sew 2 units made in Step 2 to opposite sides of each remaining unit from Step 3 to make the top and bottom diagonal rows. Press. Make 48.

6. Sew the 3 diagonal rows together. Press. Make 24 Providence blocks.

Quilt Construction

1. Sew the blocks into 6 rows of 4 blocks each. Press.

2. Sew the rows together, pressing after each addition.

3. Cut an inner border strip in half. Sew the half-strips to each of 2 long inner border strips to make 2 borders 2½″ × 60½″. Sew to the sides of the quilt. Press toward the border.

4. Cut another inner border strip in half. Sew the half-strips to each of 2 long inner border strips to make 2 borders 2½″ × 44½″. Sew to the top and bottom of the quilt. Press toward the border.

5. Make 108 quick-pieced triangle-squares:

A. Draw a solid diagonal line from corner to corner on the wrong side of each of the 54 cream outer border squares 2⅞″ × 2⅞″.

B. Pair a cream square with a blue border square 2⅞" × 2⅞", right sides facing. Sew ¼" from each side of the drawn line. Cut on the drawn line to make 2 triangle-squares. Press toward the darker fabric. Repeat with the remaining cream and blue squares to make 108.

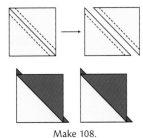

Make 108.

6. Sew 16 triangle-squares together. Repeat to make an identical row. Sew 16 triangle-squares together to make a mirror-image row. Repeat to make a second mirror-image row.

Make 2.

Make 2.

7. Sew each row to its mirror image to make 2 long borders. Sew to the sides of the quilt. Press toward the inner border.

8. Sew 11 triangle-squares together. Repeat to make an identical row. Sew 11 triangle-squares together to make a mirror-image row. Repeat to make a second mirror-image row.

9. Sew each row to its mirror image to make 2 short borders. Sew a cream border square 21/2" × 21/2" to each end of each short border.

10. Sew the short borders to the top and bottom of the quilt. Press toward the inner border.

11. Layer the quilt top, batting, and backing. Baste. Quilt as desired. Attach a hanging sleeve, if desired, and bind with the cream fabric.

Quilt Assembly Diagram

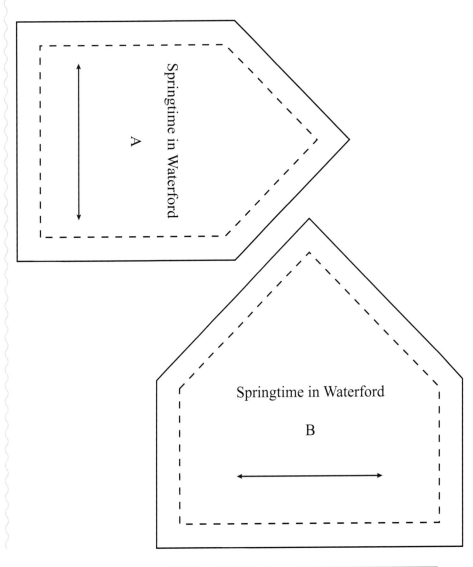

Springtime in Waterford

A

Springtime in Waterford

B

Sitting in a rocking chair near the window, her precious daughter slumbering in her arms, Judy looked up in astonishment when the quilters she had scarcely known two days before rapped softly on the open door. She beckoned them inside and, in whispers, introduced them to her husband, sleeping on the sofa, and her daughter, Emily, a beautiful girl with delicate features and a shock of silky black hair. Gwen eagerly offered to hold Emily while Judy opened her gift—and to Diane's eternal relief, Judy gasped with delight, her eyes filling with tears as she unfolded the lovely quilt. "It's beautiful," she murmured, embracing each of them in turn. "It's the most wonderful gift I've ever received. I don't know how to thank you—for this, for everything."

Excerpted from *The Winding Ways Quilt*
by Jennifer Chiaverini

Welcome, Baby Emily!

From *The Winding Ways Quilt* by Jennifer Chiaverini

Designed and pieced by Jennifer Chiaverini, machine quilted by Sue Vollbrecht, 2010.

Finished Block: Baby Bunting 8″ × 8″, Mini Baby Bunting 4″ × 4″
Finished Quilt: 40″ × 40″
Number of Blocks: 16 Baby Bunting blocks, 36 Mini Baby Bunting blocks

Materials

Red: ¾ yard (includes ⅜ yard for the binding)

Green: 1½ yards

Lavender: ½ yard

Pink: ½ yard

Gold: ½ yard

Assorted light beiges: 1¾ yards

Backing: 2⅔ yards

Batting: 48″ × 48″

Baby Bunting Cutting Instructions

Copy template patterns A and B on page 18, and pattern C on pullout page P1, onto template material.

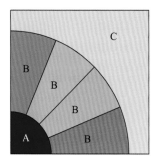

From Red

- Cut 16 A pieces.

From Green

- Cut 16 B pieces.

From Lavender

- Cut 16 B pieces.

From Pink

- Cut 16 B pieces.

From Gold

- Cut 16 B pieces.

From Assorted Light Beiges

- Cut 16 C pieces.

Baby Bunting Block Assembly

Note: Consult a general quiltmaking book if you are unfamiliar with curved piecing.

1. Sew together 1 green B, 1 gold B, 1 lavender B, and 1 pink B. Press. Repeat with the remaining B pieces to make a total of 16 pieced arcs, varying the placement of the colors for a scrappy look.

2. Matching the centers, sew a pieced arc to a red A wedge, taking care not to stretch the bias edges. Press. Repeat with the remaining red A wedges and pieced arcs.

3. Matching the centers, sew a light beige C piece to a unit created in the previous step. Press. Repeat to create 16 Baby Bunting blocks.

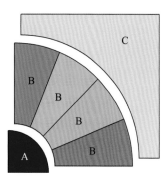

Mini Baby Bunting Cutting Instructions

Copy template patterns D, E, and F on pages 18–19 onto template material.

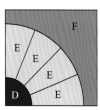

From Red

- Cut 36 D pieces.

From Assorted Light Beiges

- Cut 144 E pieces.

From Green

- Cut 36 F pieces.

Mini Baby Bunting Block Assembly

1. Sew together 4 light beige E pieces. Press. Repeat with the remaining E pieces to make a total of 36 pieced arcs.

2. Matching the centers, sew a pieced arc to a red D wedge, taking care not to stretch the bias edges. Press. Repeat with the remaining red D wedges and pieced arcs.

3. Matching the centers, sew a green F piece to a unit created in the previous step. Press. Repeat to create 36 Mini Baby Bunting blocks.

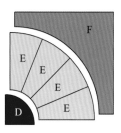

Quilt Construction

1. Sew the Baby Bunting blocks together into 4 rows of 4 blocks each, following the Quilt Assembly Diagram (page 17). Press.

2. Sew the rows together, pressing after each addition.

3. Following the Quilt Assembly Diagram carefully, sew 8 Mini Baby Bunting blocks together to make a side row. Press. Repeat to make a second side row.

4. Following the Quilt Assembly Diagram, sew 10 Mini Baby Bunting blocks together to make the top row. Press. Repeat to make the bottom row.

5. Sew the side borders to the sides of the quilt. Press.

6. Sew the top and bottom borders to the top and bottom of the quilt. Press.

7. Layer the quilt top, batting, and backing. Baste. Quilt as desired. Attach a hanging sleeve, if desired, and bind with the red fabric.

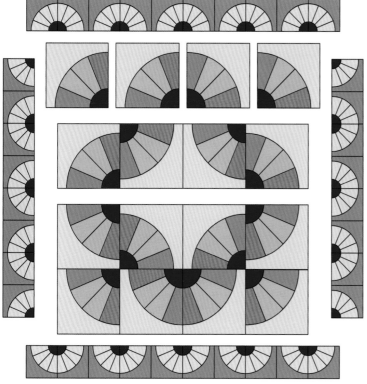

Quilt Assembly Diagram

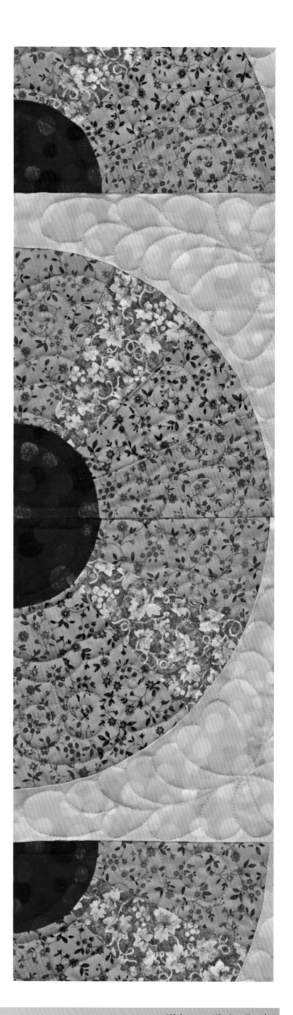

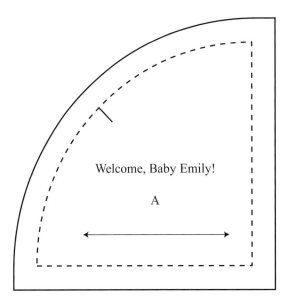

Welcome, Baby Emily!

A

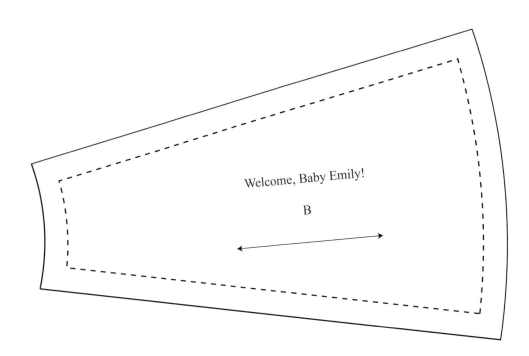

Welcome, Baby Emily!

B

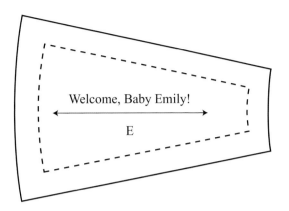

Welcome, Baby Emily!

E

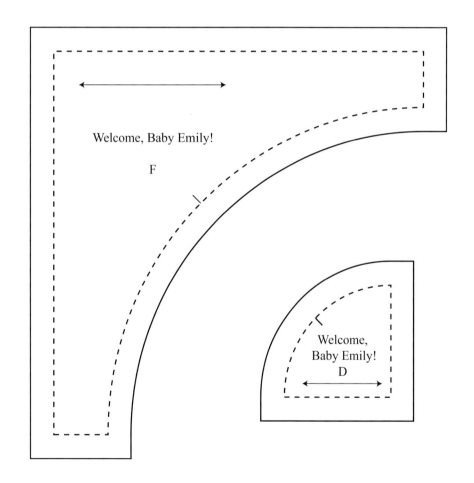

Welcome, Baby Emily!

F

Welcome,
Baby Emily!
D

FROM

The Quilter's Kitchen

In *The Quilter's Kitchen*, master quilter and founding Elm Creek Quilter Sylvia Bergstrom Compson Cooper shares the stage with newcomer Anna Del Maso, recently hired as the head chef of Elm Creek Quilt Camp. Elm Creek Manor was built in 1858, and when Anna saw the kitchen for the first time during her job interview, she was dismayed to discover that it looked every year of its age. Fortunately, Sylvia agreed that the kitchen was long overdue for an upgrade, and with camp over for the summer, the contractors are ready to begin. Sylvia and Anna must clear out the cabinets and cupboards, sorting useful items from clutter that should have been thrown out long ago. As they do, they discover cherished Bergstrom family heirlooms—an old gingham tablecloth, Great-Aunt Lydia's feed-sack aprons, a cornucopia made by Sylvia's sister, Sylvia's mother's favorite serving dish—and each unearthed treasure stirs Sylvia's memory. Special occasions Sylvia recalls include not only holidays such as Christmas, New Year's, and Thanksgiving, but also days memorable to residents of Elm Creek Manor from generations past—the annual harvest dances that brought the community together before the Second World War, the family picnics, the potlucks shared with friends and neighbors.

At the end of the novel, Anna and Sylvia decide to preserve what remains of Great-Aunt Lydia's feed-sack apron collection by piecing together its scraps into a quilt to adorn a wall of the newly remodeled kitchen. The charming wall hanging featured here, *Anna's Kitchen*, uses fabrics from my Elm Creek Quilts: The Quilter's Kitchen fabric line from Red Rooster and was inspired by the cover art and endpaper blocks from the novel.

Anna turned slowly in place, studying the kitchen and considering the possibilities. The answer was there, nearby, if she could just put her finger on it. "I've always believed that a kitchen should be the heart of the home. As the heart of Elm Creek Manor, this kitchen should preserve the past and present of the Bergstrom family and Elm Creek Quilts as no other place in the manor could."

"What do you suggest, dear?" [asked Sylvia.]

Anna's thoughts were racing so that she could barely keep up with them. "All those treasures we've discovered today, the family keepsakes that generations of Bergstroms have cherished. We need to display them here—just as we would at a Farewell Breakfast. It will be a continuous show-and-tell and sharing of memories so that everyone who enters this kitchen will know what a special place this is."

"But the tablecloth is half-ruined, and the aprons are worn almost threadbare." Suddenly Sylvia brightened. "But we don't need to save every scrap. We'll do as quilters have done since the dawn of patchwork."

All at once, Anna understood. "We'll salvage the useable pieces and sew them into a quilt."

Excerpted from *The Quilter's Kitchen*
by Jennifer Chiaverini

Anna's Kitchen

From *The Quilter's Kitchen* by Jennifer Chiaverini

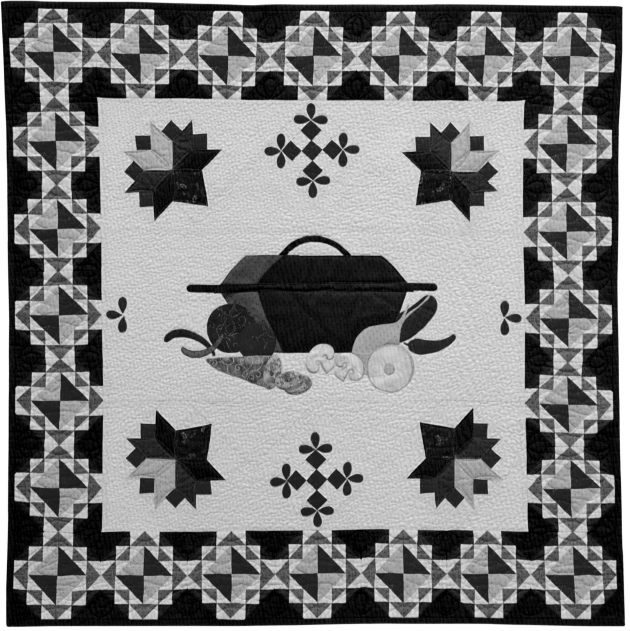

Machine pieced and appliquéd by Jennifer Chiaverini, machine quilted by Sue Vollbrecht, 2010.

Finished Block: Honeybee 5" × 5", Cornucopia 7⅛" × 7⅛", Corn and Beans 6" × 6"
Finished Quilt: 42" × 42"
Number of Blocks: 2 Honeybee blocks, 4 Cornucopia blocks, 24 Corn and Beans blocks

Cutting Instructions

Copy the appliqué template patterns on pullout pages P1–P2.

Note: Prepare the appliqués according to your favorite appliqué method. The template patterns do not include seam allowances.

Materials

Red: ½ yard

Dark red: ⅛ yard or 4½″ × 4½″ scrap

Dark blue: 1¼ yards (includes ½ yard for the binding)

Light blue: ¼ yard or 5½″ × 13″ scrap

Very dark blue: ⅛ yard or 1½″ × 19″ scrap

Dark green: ⅔ yard

Light green: ⅝ yard

Gold: ½ yard

Brown: ⅛ yard

Beige: 1¾ yards

Light beige: ¼ yard or 5″ × 9″ scrap

Orange: ⅛ yard or 4″ × 4″ scrap

Dark orange: ⅛ yard or 4″ × 10″ scrap

Backing: 2⅞ yards

Batting: 50″ × 50″

From Beige

- Cut 1 rectangle 10½″ × 20½″ for the background.

From Red

- Cut 1 circle 2⅝″ in diameter for the small tomato (N).
- Make 1 chili pepper (U).

From Dark Red

- Cut 1 circle 3⅜″ in diameter for the large tomato (L).

From Light Blue

- Make 1 lid side (B).
- Make 1 pot side (C).

From Dark Blue

- Make 1 lid front (D).
- Make 1 pot front (E).

From Very Dark Blue

- Make 2 pot handles (F).
- Make 1 lid edge (G) by cutting a strip ⅝″ × 10¾″; add the appropriate seam allowance for your favorite appliqué method and use the template to curve the ends.
- Make 1 lid handle (V).

From Dark Green

- Make 1 cucumber (A).
- Make 1 green bean (O).
- Make 1 large tomato stem (K).
- Make 1 small tomato stem (M).
- Make 1 chili pepper stem (T).

From Light Green

- Make 1 green bean (O Reverse).

From Gold

- Make 1 onion (H).
- Make 2 mushroom outlines (J).
- Cut 1 circle 3½″ in diameter for the onion slice (W).
- Cut 1 circle ¾″ in diameter for the onion slice center (X. No template; tracing a dime works well). Omit if you will be using reverse appliqué in Step 6. .

From Light Beige

● Cut 1 circle 3½" in diameter for the onion slice (W).

● Make 2 mushrooms (I).

From Orange

● Make 2 carrot slices (P).

● Make 1 sliced carrot end (R).

From Dark Orange

● Make 2 carrot slices (Q).

● Make 1 carrot (S).

Block Assembly

1. Prepare the appliqué pieces according to your favorite method. Lightly mark the placement of the appliqué shapes on the beige rectangle. Note: The lid handle, chili pepper, carrot and carrot slices, and beans will be added at the quilt assembly stage.

2. Appliqué the cucumber (A) in place.

3. Appliqué the light blue lid side (B) in place, followed by the light blue pot side (C). Next, appliqué the dark blue lid front (D) and the dark blue pot front (E). Appliqué a very dark blue pot handle (F) to each side of the pot. Appliqué the very dark blue lid edge (G), covering the raw edges of the pot, lid, and handles.

4. Appliqué the onion (H) in place.

5. Appliqué the dime-sized gold circle (X) to the center of the light beige circle (W). Note: Alternatively, cut out a dime-sized circle from the center of the light beige piece and use reverse appliqué in Step 6.

6. Appliqué the 3½"-diameter gold circle (W) in place. Appliqué the

3½"-diameter light beige circle offset slightly on top of it to complete the sliced onion. Note: If you chose reverse appliqué in the previous step, reverse appliqué the opening in the center of the light beige circle at this time. Appliqué in place.

7. Appliqué each light beige mushroom (I) to a gold mushroom outline (J). Appliqué the mushroom units in place.

8. Appliqué the large tomato stem (K) to the dark red circle (L). Appliqué the large tomato in place.

9. Appliqué the small tomato stem (M) to the red circle (N). Appliqué the small tomato in place.

10. Reverse appliqué the orange carrot slices (P) and carrot end (R) to the dark orange carrot slices (Q) and the carrot (S).

11. Set aside the lid handle (V), chili pepper (U), chili pepper stem (T), carrot (S), carrot slices (Q), and beans (O and O Reverse). They will be added during quilt construction.

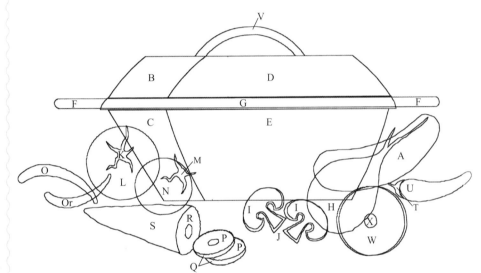

HONEYBEE

Cutting Instructions

Copy the Honeybee A appliqué template pattern A on page 30 onto the template pattern.

Note: Prepare the appliqué according to your favorite appliqué method. The template does not include seam allowances.

From Red

● Cut 1 strip 1½″ × width of fabric; subcut into 10 squares 1½″ × 1½″.

● Make 24 Honeybee A.

From Beige

● Cut 2 strips 1½″ × width of fabric; subcut into 8 squares 1½″ × 1½″, 4 rectangles 1½″ × 3½″, and 4 rectangles 1½″ × 5½″.

Block Assembly

1. Sew the red and beige squares into rows as shown. Press toward the red squares.

2. Sew the rows together to make a nine-patch. Make 2.

3. Sew the short rectangles to the sides of the nine-patches. Press. Then sew the long rectangles to the top and bottom of the nine-patches. Press.

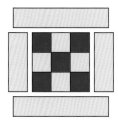

4. Appliqué the Honeybee A pieces in place as shown below and in the diagram left.

Cutting Instructions

Copy Cornucopia template patterns A, B, and E on page 30 onto template material. Transfer all the dots from the templates onto the fabric pieces.

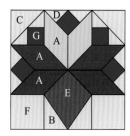

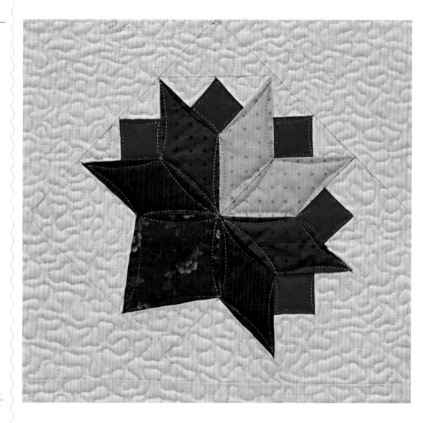

From Red

● Cut 1 strip 1½″ × width of fabric; subcut into 20 squares 1½″ × 1½″ (G).

From Gold

● Cut 8 A pieces.

From Dark Green

● Cut 8 A pieces.

From Dark Blue

● Cut 8 A pieces.

From Brown

● Cut 4 E pieces.

From Beige

● Cut 4 B triangles. Flip the template and cut 4 B Reverse triangles.

● Cut 4 squares 3″ × 3″. Cut each square in half diagonally once to make 8 C triangles.

● Cut 1 strip 2¾″ × width of fabric; subcut into 10 squares 2¾″ × 2¾″. Cut each square in half diagonally twice to make 40 D triangles.

● Cut 1 strip 2½″ × width of fabric; subcut into 8 F squares 2½″ × 2½″.

Block Assembly

Note: Consult a general quiltmaking book if you are unfamiliar with Y-seam construction.

1. Sew 2 D triangles to each red G square. Press. Make 20.

2. Sew 1 C triangle to 1 of the units from Step 1. Press. Repeat to make 8 block corners.

3. Transfer the dots on the B and E patterns to each B and E piece. Sew 1 beige B triangle and 1 beige B Reverse triangle to each brown E piece, sewing only up to the dot and backstitching. *Note: Be sure not to sew into the ¼″ seam allowances. Press.*

4. Transfer the dots on the A pattern to each A piece. Sew the gold A pieces together in pairs, sewing only from dot to dot and backstitching at each end. Make 4 pairs. Press. Sew 4 dark green A pieces to 4 dark blue pieces to make 4 pairs. Press. Sew the remaining dark green and dark blue A pieces together to make 4 mirror-image pairs. Press. Note: Be sure not to sew into the ¼″ seam allowances.

Make 4 of each.

5. Sew a unit created in Step 1 to each of the units created in Step 4. Sew only from dot to dot and backstitch at each end.

Make 4 of each.

6. Sew a gold unit to a green/blue unit. Press. Using Y-seam construction, sew a block corner into the angle. Press. Sew

a beige F square to the blue side. Press. Make 4 block halves. Note: Be sure to sew only between the dots and not into the ¼″ seam allowances.

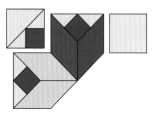

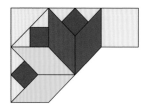

7. Sew 1 of the remaining units from Step 5 to an E unit. Press. Using Y-seam construction, sew 1 beige square (F) into the angle. Press. Sew a block corner to the green side. Press. Make 4 block halves. Note: Be sure not to sew into the ¼″ seam allowances.

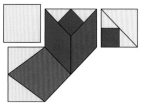

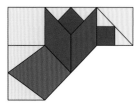

8. Pair each block half from Step 6 to a block half from Step 7 and sew together using Y-seam construction. Make 4 Cornucopia blocks.

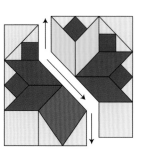

CORN AND BEANS

Cutting Instructions

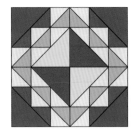

From Light Green

- Cut 7 strips 1⅞" × width of fabric; subcut into 144 squares 1⅞" × 1⅞".

From Dark Green

- Cut 5 strips 1⅞" × width of fabric; subcut into 96 squares 1⅞" × 1⅞". Cut each square in half diagonally once to make 192 triangles.

From Red

- Cut 2 strips 2⅞" × width of fabric; subcut into 24 squares 2⅞" × 2⅞". Cut each square in half diagonally once to make 48 triangles.

From Gold

- Cut 2 strips 2⅞" × width of fabric; subcut into 24 squares 2⅞" × 2⅞". Cut each square in half diagonally once to make 48 triangles.

From Dark Blue

- Cut 4 strips 2⅞" × width of fabric; subcut into 48 squares 2⅞" × 2⅞". Cut each square in half diagonally once to make 96 triangles.

From Beige

- Cut 7 strips 1⅞" × width of fabric; subcut into 144 squares 1⅞" × 1⅞".

- Cut 5 strips 1⅞" × width of fabric; subcut into 96 squares 1⅞" × 1⅞". Cut each square in half diagonally once to make 192 triangles.

Block Assembly

1. Make 288 quick-pieced half-square triangle units:

A. Draw a solid diagonal line from corner to corner on the wrong side of each beige 1⅞" × 1⅞" square.

B. Pair each beige square with a light green 1⅞" × 1⅞" square, right sides facing. Sew ¼" from each side of the drawn line. Cut on the drawn line to make 2 half-square triangle units. Press toward the darker fabric. Repeat with the remaining beige and light green squares to make 288.

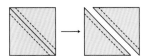

2. Sew 1 beige triangle to a beige / light green triangle-square. Press. Make 192.

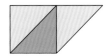

3. Sew 1 dark green triangle to a unit created in Step 2. Press. Make 96.

4. Sew 1 dark green triangle to each remaining beige / light green triangle-square. Press. Make 96.

5. Arrange the units created in Steps 2, 3, and 4 into offset rows and sew together. Press. Make 96.

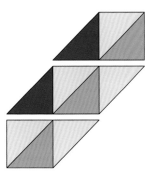

6. Sew a dark blue triangle to the dark green edge of each unit created in the previous step.

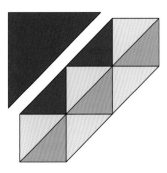

7. Sew a red triangle to half of the units created in the previous step to make 48 red quarter-blocks. Press. Sew a gold triangle to the remaining units to make 48 gold quarter-blocks. Press.

8. Pair each red quarter-block with a gold quarter-block and sew together to make 48 half-blocks. Press. Sew the half-blocks together to make 24 Corn and Beans blocks.

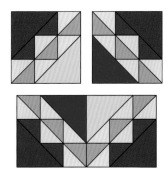

Background Cutting Instructions

From Red

● Cut 6 of Honeybee template A. This is the same template used to make the Honeybee block on page 24.

Note: Prepare the appliqué according to your favorite appliqué method. The template does not include seam allowances.

From Beige

● Cut 3 squares 8" × 8". Cut each square in half diagonally once to make 6 B setting triangles.

● Cut 2 rectangles 2⅝" × 5½" for the Honeybee block.

● Cut 2 rectangles 2⅝" × 7⅝" for the Honeybee block.

● Cut 2 squares 11¼" × 11¼". Cut each square in half diagonally twice to make 8 C setting triangles.

● Cut 2 squares 5⅞″ × 5⅞″. Cut each square in half diagonally once to make 4 D setting triangles.

Quilt Construction

1. Using the Honeybee block assembly diagram as a guide, appliqué 3 Honeybee A pieces in the corner of a B triangle. Repeat using another B and the 3 remaining Honeybee A pieces. Sew these 2 B setting triangles to opposite ends of the Kitchen Appliqué block. Press.

2. Sew 1 rectangle 2⅝″ × 5½″ to each Honeybee block. Press. Sew 1 rectangle 2⅝″ × 7⅝″ to each rectangle/Honeybee unit. Press. Sew 2 B setting triangles to each rectangle/Honeybee unit. Press.

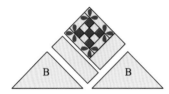

3. Sew the Honeybee units from Step 2 to the top and bottom of the Kitchen Appliqué block. Press.

4. Appliqué the pot handle, green beans, chili pepper, and carrots in place as indicated by the appliqué placement diagram.

5. Sew 2 C setting triangles to opposite sides of each Cornucopia block. Press.

6. Sew 1 D setting triangle to each Cornucopia unit. Press.

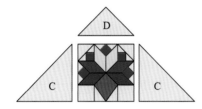

7. Sew 2 Cornucopia units to opposite sides of the Kitchen Appliqué unit. Press. Sew the remaining Cornucopia units to the other sides. Press.

8. Sew 5 Corn and Beans blocks together to make a side border. Press. Repeat to make a second side border. Sew the borders to the sides of the quilt. Press.

9. Sew 7 Corn and Beans blocks together to make a top border. Press. Repeat to make a bottom border. Sew the borders to the top and bottom of the quilt. Press.

10. Layer the quilt top, batting, and backing. Baste. Quilt as desired. Attach a hanging sleeve, if desired, and bind with the dark blue fabric.

Quilt Assembly Diagram

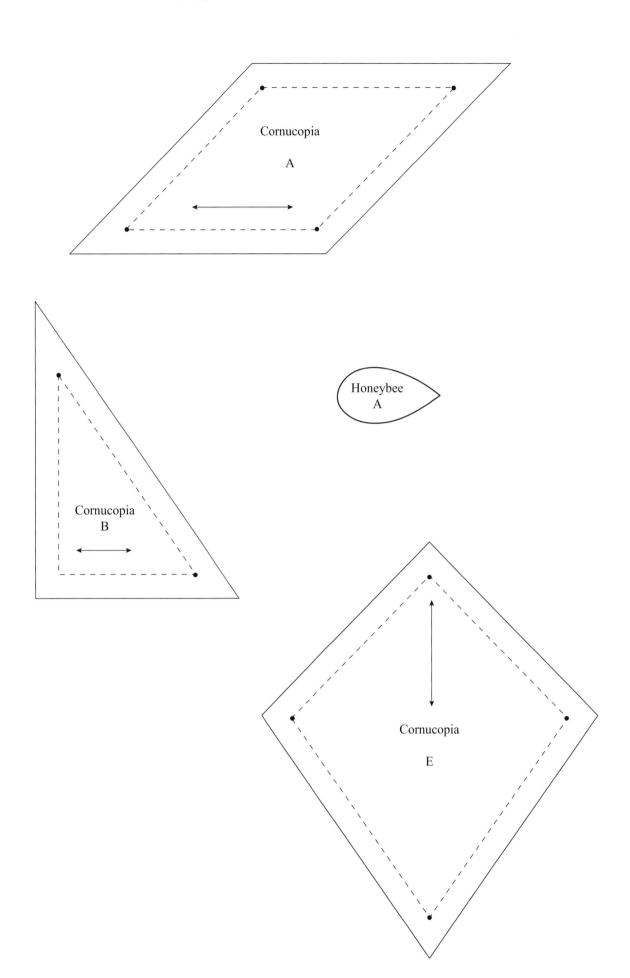

Cornucopia
A

Cornucopia
B

Honeybee
A

Cornucopia
E

FROM
The Lost Quilter

The Lost Quilter continues the story of a character introduced in *The Runaway Quilt*—Joanna, a fugitive slave who travels by the Underground Railroad to reach safe haven at Elm Creek Manor in 1859. Betrayed and recaptured, Joanna is punished for running away by being sold down south to her master's brother in South Carolina, where her needlework skills earn her the role of seamstress to the household. She marries and has a child, but she is separated from her husband and daughter when she is presented as a wedding gift to her new master's daughter. In Charleston, Joanna becomes a Union spy, for her new master is an influential Confederate officer and Joanna alone can infiltrate his study. After the great Charleston fire of 1861, Joanna takes the opportunity to escape with her children to Port Royal, where the Union is already entrenched. Many years later at a historical museum on Edisto Island, Sylvia discovers important clues about Joanna's life, bringing some closure to the mystery of the lost quilter.

The most important of these clues is an antique quilt made by a South Carolina woman known as Joanna North. Examining the quilt, a Courthouse Steps variation with an outer border of Birds in the Air blocks, Sylvia discovers fabrics identical to those in *The Runaway Quilt* made by the fugitive slave who had sought refuge at Elm Creek Farm, proving that the two Joannas were one and the same. My mother, Geraldine Neidenbach, and my sister, Heather Neidenbach, collaborated on this lovely reproduction of Joanna's quilt— *Joanna's Freedom*—using fabrics from my Elm Creek Quilts: Gerda's Collection fabric line from Red Rooster.

The second quilt, *Mr. Lincoln's Spy*, pays tribute to Joanna's role as a spy for the Union army while living in wartime Charleston. This pattern originally appeared in the August/September 2010 issue of *Country Woman* magazine, and I thank the publisher for allowing me to include it in this book.

At last Sophia brought the tour to a stop before what appeared to be the oldest quilt in the collection. Though the pieces were worn and faded, the pattern had retained its striking boldness—a Courthouse Steps variation surrounded by an outer border of solid squares occasionally replaced by a Birds in the Air block. Beside her, Sylvia heard Sarah draw in a sharp breath of recognition and excitement.

"We're certain that Joanna North herself made this quilt," Sophia said proudly, pleased by Sarah's reaction, though she could not possibly suspect its cause. "It's the jewel of our collection."

"How do you know Joanna made it?" asked Sarah, although she surely knew that Sophia's conclusion was true.

Surely Sarah must have recognized the size of the Birds in the Air blocks, the blue-and-brown homespun fabric used in the large triangle in the lower right corner, the double pinks scattered here and there in the smaller triangles, the dark wools, the soft faded cottons. Sylvia had known them the moment she saw them, for she had seen those same prints and patterns in another quilt, studied them and wondered about them and the woman who had sewn the small pieces together for so long that they were engraved on her memory.

"Yes, how can you be sure?" Justine asked. "Did Joanna sign the quilt or embroider her initials?"

"She wrote about it in her journal," Sophia explained. "One of the few extant complete passages describes how she enlarged a quilt that had turned out too small by attaching borders made from blocks left over from an earlier project. I only wish our collection boasted that first quilt, the quilt that influenced all the Quilts of North Freedom that followed, but I'm afraid that treasure has been lost to history."

"Perhaps it's not lost after all," said Sylvia, beckoning Sarah to open the tote bag, to show Sophia the tattered Birds in the Air quilt that had set her upon a quest to discover what had happened to Gerda's lost quilter, a quest that seemed, at last, to have reached its end.

Excerpted from *The Lost Quilter*
by Jennifer Chiaverini

Joanna's Freedom

From *The Lost Quilter* by Jennifer Chiaverini

Designed by Jennifer Chiaverini, pieced by Heather Neidenbach and Geraldine Neidenbach,
machine quilted by Sue Vollbrecht, 2010.

Finished Block: Courthouse Steps 7″ × 7″, half Courthouse Steps 3½″ × 7″, Birds in the Air 4½″ × 4½″

Finished Quilt: 54″ × 72″

Number of Blocks: 48 Courthouse Steps blocks, 12 Courthouse Steps half-blocks, 52 Birds in the Air blocks

Materials

Medium blue: ¼ yard

Assorted dark blue prints: 1¾ yards total (includes ½ yard for the binding)

Assorted red prints: 1¼ yards total

Assorted brown prints: 1¼ yards total

Assorted gold prints: ¾ yard total

Assorted beige tone-on-tones: 2⅜ yards total

Beige tone-on-tone for inner border: ⅓ yard

Backing: 3¾ yards

Batting: 62″ × 80″

Courthouse Steps Cutting Instructions

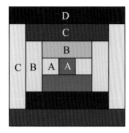

From Medium Blue

- Cut 3 strips 1½″ × width of fabric; subcut into 60 squares 1½″ × 1½″ (A).

From Assorted Dark Blue Prints

- Cut 27 rectangles 1½″ × 3½″ (B).
- Cut 27 rectangles 1½″ × 5½″ (C).
- Cut 24 rectangles 1½″ × 7½″ (D).

From Assorted Red Prints

- Cut 27 rectangles 1½″ × 3½″ (B).
- Cut 27 rectangles 1½″ × 5½″ (C).
- Cut 24 rectangles 1½″ × 7½″ (D).

From Assorted Brown Prints

- Cut 27 rectangles 1½″ × 3½″ (B).
- Cut 27 rectangles 1½″ × 5½″ (C).
- Cut 24 rectangles 1½″ × 7½″ (D).

From Assorted Gold Prints

- Cut 27 rectangles 1½″ × 3½″ (B).
- Cut 27 rectangles 1½″ × 5½″ (C).
- Cut 24 rectangles 1½″ × 7½″ (D).

From Assorted Beige Tone-on-Tones

- Cut 120 squares 1½″ × 1½″ (A).
- Cut 24 rectangles 1½″ × 2½″ (E).
- Cut 120 rectangles 1½″ × 3½″ (B).
- Cut 96 rectangles 1½″ × 5½″ (C).
- Cut 12 rectangles 1″ × 7½″ (F).

Courthouse Steps Block Assembly

1. Sew 2 beige A squares to opposite sides of each medium blue A square. Press toward the medium blue fabric. Make 60. Set aside 12 for the Courthouse Steps half-blocks.

2. Sew 2 dark blue, red, brown, or gold B rectangles to opposite sides of 48 of the units created in the previous step. Press. Varying the color placement to create a scrappy look, repeat with the remaining units to make 48.

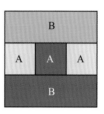

3. Sew 2 beige B rectangles to opposite sides of the units created in the previous step. Press. Make 48.

4. Continuing in a similar fashion and varying the color placement of the dark fabrics, add the dark C rectangles, the beige C rectangles, and the dark D rectangles, pressing after each addition. Make 48 Courthouse Steps blocks.

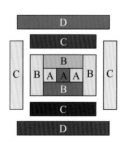

5. Sew a dark B rectangle to a side of a remaining blue/beige square unit created in Step 1. Press. Sew 2 beige E rectangles to opposite ends. Press. Sew a dark C rectangle to a side of the unit. Press. Sew 2 beige B rectangles to opposite ends. Press. Attach an F rectangle. Press. Repeat to make 12 Courthouse Steps half-blocks.

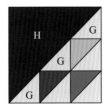

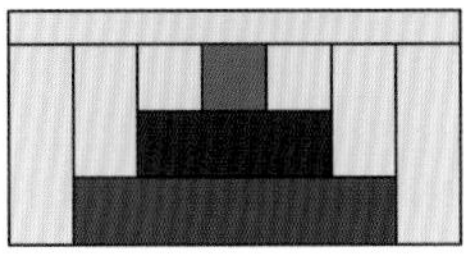

Birds in the Air Cutting Instructions

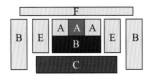

From Assorted Dark Blue Prints

● Cut 9 squares 5⅜″ × 5⅜″. Cut each square in half diagonally once to make 18 H triangles.

● Cut 20 squares 2⅜″ × 2⅜″.

From Assorted Red Prints

● Cut 9 squares 5⅜″ × 5⅜″. Cut each square in half diagonally once to make 18 H triangles.

● Cut 20 squares 2⅜″ × 2⅜″.

From Assorted Brown Prints

● Cut 8 squares 5⅜″ × 5⅜″. Cut each square in half diagonally once to make 16 H triangles.

● Cut 20 squares 2⅜″ × 2⅜″.

From Assorted Gold Prints

● Cut 18 squares 2⅜″ × 2⅜″.

From Assorted Beige Tone-on-Tones

● Cut 78 squares 2⅜″ × 2⅜″.

● Cut 78 squares 2⅜″ × 2⅜″. Cut each square in half diagonally once to make 156 G triangles.

From Beige Tone-on-Tone for Inner Border

● Cut 4 strips 2″ × width of fabric. Pair the strips and sew them end to end to make 2 long strips (set aside for the inner side borders).

Birds in the Air Block Assembly

1. Make 156 quick-pieced half-square triangle units:

A. Draw a solid diagonal line from corner to corner on the wrong side of each 2⅜″ × 2⅜″ beige square.

B. Pair a beige square with a dark (blue, red, brown, or gold) 2⅜″ × 2⅜″ square, right sides facing. Sew ¼″ from each side of the drawn line. Cut on the solid line to make 2 half-square triangle units. Press toward the darker fabric. Repeat with the remaining beige squares and dark squares to make 156.

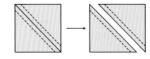

2. Set aside 52 quick-pieced half-square triangle units in assorted colors. Sew the remaining half-square triangle units together in pairs, varying the color placement. Press. Sew 1 beige G triangle to each pair. Press. Make 52 units.

3. Sew 2 beige G triangles to each remaining half-square triangle unit. Press. Make 52.

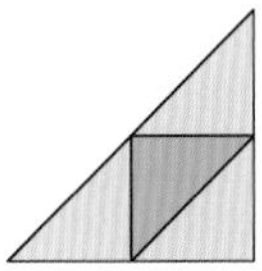

4. Sew each unit from Step 2 to a unit from Step 3. Press. Make 52.

5. Sew each unit from Step 4 to a dark H triangle. Press. Make 52 Birds in the Air blocks.

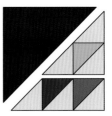

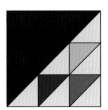

Quilt Construction

1. Sew the Courthouse Steps blocks into 8 rows of 6 blocks each. Press.

2. Sew the rows together, pressing after each addition.

3. Sew the Courthouse Steps half-blocks together into 2 rows of 6 blocks each. Press.

4. Sew 1 of the half-block rows to the top of the quilt and 1 to the bottom. Press.

5. Sew the inner borders to the sides of the quilt. Trim excess. Press toward the beige fabric.

6. Following the Quilt Assembly Diagram for the orientation of the blocks, sew 7 Birds in the Air blocks together. Repeat to make an identical row. Sew 7 Birds in the Air blocks together to make a mirror-image row. Repeat to make a second mirror-image row.

7. Sew each row to its mirror image to make 2 side borders. Press. Sew the borders to the sides of the quilt. Press toward the inner border.

8. Following the Quilt Assembly Diagram for the orientation of the blocks, sew 6 Birds in the Air blocks together. Repeat to make an identical row. Sew 6 Birds in the Air blocks together to make a mirror-image row. Repeat to make a second mirror-image row.

9. Sew each row to its mirror image to make the top and bottom borders. Press. Sew the short borders to the top and bottom of the quilt. Press toward the inner border.

10. Layer the quilt top, batting, and backing. Baste. Quilt as desired. Attach a hanging sleeve, if desired, and bind with dark blue fabric.

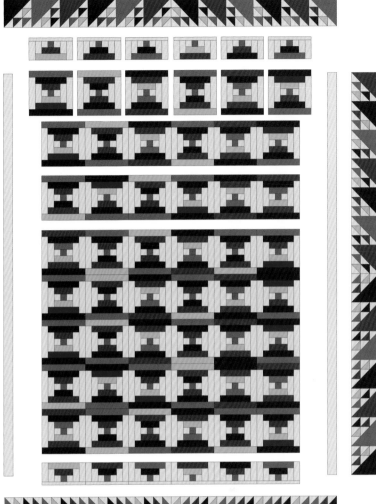

Quilt Assembly Diagram

Mr. Lincoln's Spy

From *The Lost Quilter* by Jennifer Chiaverini

Designed and pieced by Jennifer Chiaverini, machine quilted by Sue Vollbrecht, 2009.

Finished Block: Lincoln 10″ × 10″, border 4″ × 4″

Finished Quilt: 52″ × 72″

Number of Blocks: 24 Lincoln blocks, 58 border blocks

Materials

Green pin dot: 1⅜ yards (includes ⅝ yard for the binding)

Stripe: 1 yard

Red pin dot: ⅝ yard

Beige tone-on-tone: 2 yards

Leaves and berries print: ¾ yard

Gold pin dot: 1 yard

Backing: 3½ yards

Batting: 60″ × 80″

Block Cutting Instructions

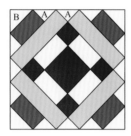

From Green Pin Dot

- Cut 2 strips 3⅜″ × width of fabric.
- Cut 6 strips 1⅞″ × width of fabric.

From Stripe (Stripes Parallel to Selvage)

- Cut 5 strips 6⅛″ × width of fabric; subcut into 96 rectangles 1⅞″ × 6⅛″.

Note: If the stripes in your fabric are perpendicular to the selvage, cut 16 strips 1⅞″ × width of fabric and cut 96 rectangles 1⅞″ × 6⅛″.

From Red Pin Dot

- Cut 5 strips 3⅜″ × width of fabric; subcut into 96 rectangles 1⅞″ × 3⅜″.

From Beige Tone-on-Tone

- Cut 3 strips 3⅜″ × width of fabric.
- Cut 4 strips 1⅞″ × width of fabric.
- Cut 6 strips 3¼″ × width of fabric; subcut into 72 squares 3¼″ × 3¼″. Cut each square in half diagonally twice to make 288 A triangles.
- Cut 4 strips 2⅞″ × width of fabric; subcut into 48 squares 2⅞″ × 2⅞″. Cut each square in half diagonally once to make 96 B triangles.

Block Assembly

1. Sew 2 green 1⅞″ strips to the long sides of 1 beige 3⅜″ strip to make a strip set. Press toward the green fabric. Repeat to make 3 strip sets. Cut the strip sets into 48 segments 1⅞″ wide.

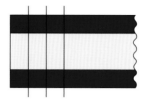

2. Sew 2 beige 1⅞″ strips to the long sides of 1 green 3⅜″ strip to make a strip set. Press toward the green fabric. Repeat to make 2 strip sets. Cut the strip sets into 24 segments 3⅜″ wide.

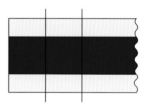

3. Sew 2 segments created in Step 1 to the top and bottom of each segment created in Step 2 to make 24 asymmetrical nine-patches. Press the seams open.

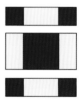

4. Sew 2 beige A triangles to the ends of each red rectangle. Press toward the red fabric. Repeat to make 96 units.

5. Sew a stripe rectangle to the base of a red rectangle unit created in Step 4. Sew a beige B triangle to the top. Press. Repeat to make a total of 48 corner unit 1s.

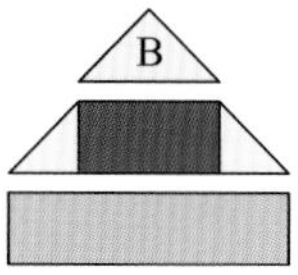

6. Sew 2 beige A triangles to the ends of the remaining 48 stripe rectangles. Press toward the stripe fabric.

7. Sew a red rectangle unit created in Step 4 to a stripe rectangle unit created in Step 6. Sew a beige triangle B to the top of the unit. Press. Repeat to make a total of 48 corner unit 2s.

8. Sew 2 corner unit 1s to opposite sides of a nine-patch unit. Press. Repeat to make 24.

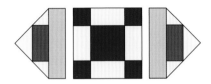

9. Sew 2 corner unit 2s to opposite sides of a unit created in Step 8. Press. Repeat to make 24 Union blocks.

Border Cutting Instructions

From Leaves and Berries

● Cut 6 strips 3⅜″ × width of fabric; subcut into 58 D squares 3⅜″ × 3⅜″.

From Gold Pin Dot

● Cut 9 strips 2⅞″ × width of fabric; subcut into 116 squares 2⅞″ × 2⅞″. Cut each square in half once diagonally to make 232 C triangles.

From Beige Tone-on-Tone

● Cut 7 strips 2½″ × width of fabric.

Border Assembly

1. Sew 2 C triangles to opposite sides of a D square. Press toward the square.

2. Sew 2 C triangles to the remaining sides of the D square to make a border block. Press. Repeat to make a total of 58 border blocks.

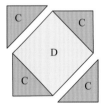

3. Sew 16 border blocks together to make a side border. Press. Repeat to make a second side border.

4. Sew 13 border blocks together to make a top border. Press. Repeat to make a bottom border.

Quilt Construction

1. Sew 4 Lincoln blocks together to make 1 row. Press. Repeat to make 6 rows.

2. Sew the 6 rows together. Press.

3. Sew 4 border strips end to end in pairs to make 2 inner borders. Sew the 2 inner borders to the sides of the quilt. Press toward the inner border. Trim excess.

4. Cut a border strip in half and sew each half to a remaining inner border strip. Sew 2 inner borders to the top and bottom of the quilt. Press toward the inner border. Trim excess.

5. Sew the 2 pieced side borders to the sides of the quilt. Press toward the inner borders.

6. Sew the 2 pieced top and bottom borders to the top and bottom of the quilt. Press toward the inner borders.

7. Layer the quilt top, batting, and backing. Baste. Quilt as desired. Attach a hanging sleeve, if desired, and bind with the green pin dot fabric.

Quilt Assembly Diagram

FROM
A Quilter's Holiday

For the Elm Creek Quilters, the day after Thanksgiving marks the start of the holiday quilting season, a time to gather at Elm Creek Manor and spend the day stitching holiday gifts for loved ones. This year, in keeping with the season's spirit of gratitude, master quilter Sylvia Bergstrom Compson Cooper is eager to revive a cherished family tradition. A recent remodeling of the manor's kitchen unearthed a cornucopia that once served as the centerpiece of the Bergstrom family's holiday table. Into it, each Bergstrom would place an object that symbolized something he or she was especially thankful for that year. On this quilter's holiday, Sylvia has invited her friends to continue the tradition by sewing quilt blocks that represent their thankfulness and gratitude.

As each quilter explains the significance of her carefully chosen block, stories emerge of love and longing for family and friends, feelings also expressed in the gifts they work upon throughout the day. *Cornucopia of Thanks* is a sampler of the gratitude blocks the Elm Creek Quilters place into

the cornucopia centerpiece as well as a few others from the holiday quilts they work upon during their Quilter's Holiday sewing bee.

As an early winter storm blankets Elm Creek Manor in heavy snow, Gwen Sullivan, a professor of American Studies at nearby Waterford College, hopes to finish a quilt begun by her graduate school mentor. Victoria Stark had intended the quilt as a gift of gratitude for her bone marrow donor, but when illness prevented her from completing it, she asked Gwen to finish it in time for Christmas. *Remembering Victoria* features the Augusta block and is made from my Elm Creek Quilts: Joanna's Collection fabric line from Red Rooster.

Sylvia's task for that Quilter's Holiday is to make a quilt to sell at her church's Holiday Boutique, a fundraiser for a local food pantry. Chimneys and Cornerstones blocks frame Star of the Magi blocks, and the rich red, green, gold, and purple fabrics add the perfect seasonal touch to *Holiday Blessings*.

Cornucopia of Thanks

From *A Quilter's Holiday* by Jennifer Chiaverini

Designed by Jennifer Chiaverini, pieced by Jennifer Chiaverini and Geraldine Neidenbach,
machine quilted by Sue Vollbrecht, 2010.

Finished Block: 12″ × 12″

Finished Quilt: 72″ × 90″

Number of Blocks: 12 blocks

Materials

Dark green: 2¼ yards

Medium green: ⅔ yard

Dark rust: 3¼ yards (includes ¾ yard
for the binding)

Gold: 1¾ yards

Dark purple: ¼ yard

Medium purple: ¾ yard

Cream: 2⅛ yards

Backing: 5½ yards

Batting: 80″ × 98″

Cutting Instructions

Copy Remembering Victoria
*Augusta template patterns A, B,
and C on page 63 onto template
material.*

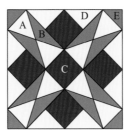

From Medium Purple

- Cut 8 B pieces.

- Cut 2 squares 2⅞″ × 2⅞″. Cut each
square in half diagonally once to
make 4 E triangles.

From Dark Rust

- Cut 5 C pieces.

From Cream

- Cut 8 A pieces.

- Cut 2 squares 5¼″ × 5¼″. Cut each
square in half diagonally twice to
make 8 D triangles.

Block Assembly

Follow the *Remembering Victoria*
Augusta block assembly instructions on
pages 61–62 to make 1 Augusta block.

Cutting Instructions

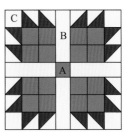

From Medium Purple

- Cut 1 square 2″ × 2″ (A).

- Cut 1 strip 2¼″ × 22″.

From Medium Green

- Cut 1 strip 2¼″ × 22″.

From Dark Rust

- Cut 8 squares 2⅝″ × 2⅝″.

From Cream

- Cut 4 rectangles 2″ × 5¾″ (B).

- Cut 4 squares 2¼″ × 2¼″ (C).

- Cut 8 squares 2⅝″ × 2⅝″.

Block Assembly

1. Sew the medium purple strip to the
medium green strip. Press toward
the medium purple fabric. With your
rotary cutter, crosscut 8 segments
2¼″ wide.

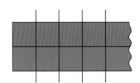

2. Abutting the seams and aligning
different colors, sew the segments
together to make 4 four-patches.

3. Make 16 quick-pieced dark rust and cream triangle-squares:

A. Draw a diagonal line from corner to corner on the wrong side of each 2⅝″ × 22⅝″ cream square.

B. Pair a cream square with a dark rust 2⅝″ × 22⅝″ square, right sides facing. Sew ¼″ from each side of the drawn line.

C. Cut on the drawn line to make 2 triangle-squares. Press toward the dark rust fabric. Repeat with the remaining cream and dark rust 2⅝″ × 2›″ squares to make 16 triangle-squares.

4. Sew the triangle-squares together in pairs to make 4 units and 4 mirror-image units. Press.

5. Sew 1 triangle-square unit to each four-patch. Press.

6. Sew 1 cream C square to an end of each mirror-image triangle-square unit. Press.

7. Sew 1 unit created in Step 6 to 1 unit created in Step 5. Press. Repeat to make 4.

8. Sew 2 of the units created in Step 7 to opposite sides of a cream B rectangle to make the top row. Press. Repeat to make the bottom row.

9. Sew the remaining cream B rectangles to opposite sides of the medium purple A square. Press.

10. Sew the 3 rows together. Press.

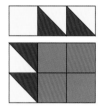

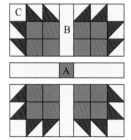

CORNUCOPIA

Cutting Instructions

Copy **Cornucopia of Thanks** *Cornucopia template patterns A, B, and E on pages 55 and 58 onto template material.*

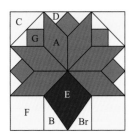

From Medium Purple

- Cut 5 squares 2¼″ × 2¼″ (G).

From Medium Green

- Cut 6 A pieces.

From Dark Rust

- Cut 1 E piece.

From Cream

- Cut 1 B triangle. Flip the template and cut 1 B Reverse triangle.

- Cut 1 square 4⅜″ × 4⅜″. Cut the square in half diagonally once to make 2 C triangles.

- Cut 3 squares 3¾″ × 3¾″. Cut each square in half diagonally twice to make 12 D triangles. (You will need only 10.)

- Cut 2 squares 4″ × 4″ (F).

Block Assembly

Follow the assembly instructions on pages 25–26 to make 1 Cornucopia block.

GRANDMOTHER'S DELIGHT

Cutting Instructions

Copy **Cornucopia of Thanks** *Grandmother's Delight template patterns A, B, and C on pages 54, 55 and 57 onto template material.*

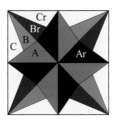

From Medium Purple

- Cut 4 A triangles.

From Dark Purple

- Flip over template A and cut 4 A Reverse triangles.

From Gold

- Cut 4 B triangles.

From Dark Rust

- Flip over template B and cut 4 B Reverse triangles.

From Cream

- Cut 4 C triangles.

- Flip over template C and cut 4 C Reverse triangles.

Block Assembly

1. Sew each B triangle to a C triangle. Press.

2. Sew an A triangle to each unit created in Step 1. Press.

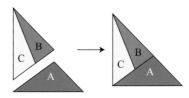

3. Sew each B Reverse triangle to a C Reverse triangle. Press.

4. Sew an A Reverse triangle to each unit created in Step 3. Press.

5. Sew each A/B/C unit to an A/B/C Reverse unit. Press.

6. Following the block assembly diagram, sew the units created in the previous steps into rows. Press. Sew the rows together. Press.

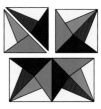

GUIDING STAR

Cutting Instructions

Copy Cornucopia of Thanks Guiding Star template patterns A–F on pages 54–58 onto template material.

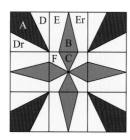

From Dark Rust

- Cut 4 A pieces.

From Medium Purple

- Cut 4 B triangles.
- Cut 4 C triangles.

From Cream

- Cut 4 D triangles. Flip the template and cut 4 D Reverse triangles.
- Cut 4 E pieces. Flip the template and cut 4 E Reverse pieces.
- Cut 4 F pieces.

Block Assembly

1. Sew 1 cream D and 1 cream D Reverse to each dark rust A to make 4 block corners. Press.

2. Sew 1 cream E and 1 cream E Reverse to each medium purple B to make 4 block sides. Press.

3. Sew 1 cream F to 1 medium purple C. Press. Repeat to make 4.

4. Sew 2 of the units created in Step 3 together. Press. Repeat with the remaining units.

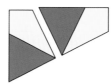

5. Sew the units created in Step 4 together to make the block center. Press.

6. Following the block assembly diagram, sew the segments into 3 rows. Press. Sew the rows together. Press.

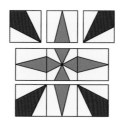

NINE-PATCH

Cutting Instructions

From Dark Rust

- Cut 5 squares 4½" × 4½".

From Cream

- Cut 4 squares 4½" × 4½".

Block Assembly

1. Sew 2 dark rust squares to opposite sides of a cream square. Press toward the dark rust squares. Repeat to make a second identical row.

2. Sew 2 cream squares to opposite sides of the remaining dark rust square. Press toward the dark rust square.

3. Abut the seams and sew the 3 rows together. Press.

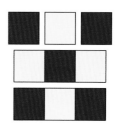

PROSPERITY

Cutting Instructions

Copy Cornucopia of Thanks *Prosperity template patterns C, E, F, and G on pages 53–58 onto template material. Transfer all the dots from the templates onto the fabric pieces.*

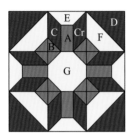

From Medium Green

- Cut 4 rectangles 1¾" × 3⅛" (A).
- Cut 8 squares 2¼" × 2¼". Cut each square in half once diagonally to make 16 B triangles.

From Dark Rust

- Cut 4 C pieces. Flip the template and make 4 C Reverse pieces.
- Cut 2 squares 4⅞" × 4⅞". Cut each square in half once diagonally to make 4 D triangles.

From Cream

- Make 4 E trapezoids.
- Make 4 F trapezoids.
- Make 1 G octagon.

Block Assembly

Note: Consult a general quiltmaking book if you are unfamiliar with Y-seam construction.

1. Sew 4 green B triangles to opposite long sides of the cream G octagon to make the block center. Press.

2. Sew 1 green B triangle to 1 short side of each C and each C Reverse. Repeat to make 4 B/C units and 4 B / C Reverse units. Press.

3. Taking care not to sew into the seam allowance by sewing only to the marked dot and backstitching, sew 1 C unit and 1 C Reverse unit to opposite sides of a green A rectangle. Press. Using Y-seam construction, sew an E trapezoid between the star points, again sewing only between the dots and then from each dot to the edge. Press. Repeat to make 4 identical units.

4. Sew 1 dark rust D triangle and 1 medium green B triangle to each cream F trapezoid. Press. Repeat to make 4 identical units.

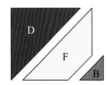

5. Following the block assembly diagram, arrange the units into 3 rows and sew. Press. Sew the 3 rows together. Press.

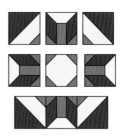

PROVIDENCE

Cutting Instructions

Copy Cornucopia of Thanks *Providence template patterns A–E on pages 54–58 onto template material.*

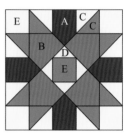

From Dark Rust

- Cut 4 A pieces.

From Medium Green

- Cut 4 B pieces.

From Medium Purple

- Cut 8 C triangles.
- Cut 1 E square.

From Cream

- Cut 8 C triangles.
- Cut 4 D triangles.
- Cut 4 E squares.

Block Assembly

Follow the *Springtime in Waterford* Providence block assembly instructions on page 12 to make 1 Providence block.

SIGNS OF SPRING

Cutting Instructions

Copy Cornucopia of Thanks *Signs of Spring* template patterns A and D on pullout page P4 onto template material. Transfer all the dots from the templates onto the fabric pieces.

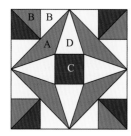

From Medium Green

- Cut 4 A triangles.

- Cut 2 squares 3⅞″ × 3⅞″. Cut each square in half once diagonally to make 4 B triangles.

From Dark Rust

- Cut 1 square 3½″ × 3½″ (C).

- Cut 2 squares 3⅞″ × 3⅞″. Cut each square in half once diagonally to make 4 B triangles.

From Cream

- Make 4 D triangles.

- Cut 4 squares 3⅞″ × 3⅞″. Cut each square in half once diagonally to make 8 B triangles.

Block Assembly

Note: Consult a general quiltmaking book if you are unfamiliar with Y-seam construction.

1. Pair each medium green B triangle with a dark rust B triangle and sew along the longest edge to make 4 triangle-squares. Press.

2. Sew 2 cream B triangles to adjacent sides of each triangle-square to make 4 block corners. Press.

3. Sew the 4 D cream triangles to the dark rust C square, taking care to sew only from dot to dot, not into the seam allowance. Backstitch at each end. Press.

4. Using Y-seam construction, sew 2 medium green A triangles to opposite sides of the unit created in the previous step, taking care to sew only from the dot to the edge and not into the inner seam allowance. Backstitch at each end. Press. Attach the remaining 2 medium green A triangles to complete the block center. Press.

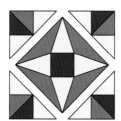

5. Sew 2 block corners to opposite sides of the block center. Press. Sew on the remaining 2 block corners. Press.

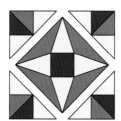

STAR OF THE MAGI

Cutting Instructions

Copy Holiday Blessings *Star of the Magi* template patterns A–C on page 70 onto template material. Transfer all the dots from the templates onto the fabric pieces.

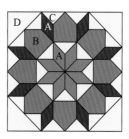

From Medium Purple

- Cut 8 A pieces.

From Dark Rust

- Cut 8 A pieces.

From Medium Green

- Cut 8 B pieces.

From Cream

- Cut 16 C triangles.

- Cut 2 squares 4⅜″ × 4⅜″. Cut each square in half diagonally once to make 4 D triangles.

Block Assembly

Follow the Star of the Magi assembly instructions on pages 66–67 to make 1 Star of the Magi block.

SWAMP PATCH

Cutting Instructions

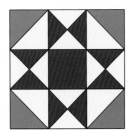

From Medium Purple

- Cut 2 squares 4⅞″ × 4⅞″.

From Dark Rust

- Cut 1 square 4½″ × 4½″.
- Cut 2 squares 5¼″ × 5¼″.

From Cream

- Cut 2 squares 4⅞″ × 4⅞″.
- Cut 2 squares 5¼″ × 5¼″.

Block Assembly

1. Make 4 quick-pieced medium purple and cream triangle-squares:

A. Draw a diagonal line from corner to corner on the wrong side of each 4⅞″ × 4⅞″ cream square.

B. Pair a cream square with a medium purple square, right sides facing. Sew ¼″ from each side of the drawn line.

C. Cut on the drawn line to make 2 triangle-squares. Press toward the medium purple fabric. Repeat with the remaining medium purple and cream 4⅞″ × 4⅞″ squares to make 4 triangle-squares.

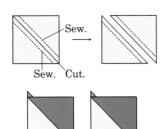

2. Make 4 quick-pieced quarter-square triangle units:

A. Using the 5¼″ × 5¼″ dark rust and cream squares, follow the sewing and cutting instructions in Step 1 to make 4 triangle-squares.

B. On the wrong side of 1 triangle-square, draw a diagonal line from a dark rust corner to a cream corner.

C. Place 2 half-square triangle units together, with right sides facing and with dark rust triangles facing cream triangles. Align the edges, abut the opposing seams, and pin. Sew ¼″ from each side of the drawn line.

D. Cut on the drawn line to make 2 quarter-square triangle units. Press. Repeat with the remaining triangle-squares to make 2 more quarter-square triangle units.

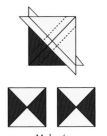

Make 4.

3. Following the block assembly diagram, arrange the triangle-squares, quarter-square triangle units, and dark rust square into 3 rows and sew. Press. Sew the 3 rows together. Press.

TWIN STAR

Star Cutting Instructions

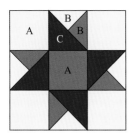

From Medium Purple

- Cut 1 square 4½″ × 4½″ (A).

- Cut 1 square 5¼″ × 5¼″. Cut in half diagonally twice to make 4 B triangles.

From Dark Rust

- Cut 2 squares 4⅞″ × 4⅞″. Cut each square in half diagonally once to make 4 C triangles.

From Cream

- Cut 4 squares 4½″ × 4½″ (A).

- Cut 1 square 5¼″ × 5¼″. Cut in half diagonally twice to make 4 B triangles.

Block Assembly

1. Pair each medium purple B triangle with a cream B triangle and sew along a short side to make 4 identical medium purple triangle points. Press.

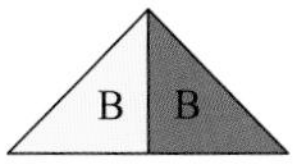

Make 4.

2. Pair each medium purple triangle point with a dark rust C triangle and sew along the longest edge. Press.

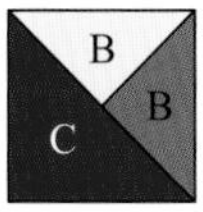

Make 4.

3. Following the block assembly diagram, arrange the block segments into 3 rows and sew. Press. Sew the 3 rows together. Press.

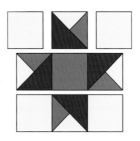

Background Cutting Instructions

From Gold:

- Cut 1 strip 3¼″ × width of fabric; subcut into 6 squares 3¼″ × 3¼″ for the cornerstones.

- Cut 2 strips 5¼″ × width of fabric; subcut into 12 squares 5¼″ × 5¼″. Cut each square in half diagonally twice to make 48 gold triangles (34 for the sashing and 14 for the outer sashing).

- Cut 7 strips 3½″ × width of fabric for the border.

From Cream:

- Cut 3 strips 1¼″ × width of fabric; subcut into 12 rectangles 1¼″ × 3¼″ and 12 rectangles 1¼″ × 4¾″ for the cornerstones.

- Cut 16 strips 1¼″ × width of fabric for the sashing and outer sashing.

From Dark Green:

- Cut 2 strips 3⅞″ × width of fabric; subcut into 12 squares 3⅞″ × 3⅞″ for the cornerstones.

- Cut 2 strips 3⅞″ × width of fabric; subcut into 14 squares 3⅞″ × 3⅞″. Cut each square once diagonally to make 28 dark green triangles for the outer sashing.

- Cut 2 strips 7¼″ × width of fabric; subcut into 9 squares 7¼″ × 7¼″. Cut each square in half diagonally twice to make 34 dark green triangles for the sashing (there will be 2 left over).

- Cut 11 strips 3½″ × width of fabric; subcut into 34 rectangles 3½″ × 6½″ for the sashing. With the rest, make the outer sashing: Cut 10 rectangles 3½″ × 12½″, 4 rectangles 3½″ × 6½″, and 4 squares 3½″ × 3½″.

From Dark Rust Fabric:

- Cut 8 strips 6½″ × width of fabric.

Quilt Assembly

1. Make 6 setting cornerstones:

   A. Sew 2 cream rectangles 1¼″ × 3¼″ to opposite sides of each gold 3¼″ × 3¼″ square. Press.

   B. Sew 2 long 1¼″ × 4¾″ rectangles to the remaining opposite sides of each gold square. Press.

   C. Sew 2 dark green 3⅞″ triangles to opposite sides of each gold/cream unit. Press. Sew 2 dark green triangles to the remaining sides of each gold/cream unit. Press.

Make 6.

2. Make 17 pieced sashing units:

   A. Sew a 1¼″-wide cream strip to the left short leg of a gold 5¼″ triangle, matching the end of the strip to the right angle but extending the strip at least ¼″ beyond the base before trimming the excess fabric. Press. Sew another cream strip to the other short leg of the triangle, again extending the strip ¼″ beyond the base before trimming the excess fabric. Press. Carefully trim the excess fabric to make a right triangle with a base of 7¼″. Repeat to make 34.

   B. Sew 1 dark green 7¼″ triangle to each of the gold/cream triangle units. Press toward the dark green triangle. Make 34.

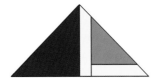

   C. Sew the units created in Step 2B together in pairs. Press. Make 17.

   D. Sew 2 dark green 3½″ × 6½″ rectangles to opposite sides of each unit created in Step 2C. Press toward the dark green rectangles. Make 17.

3. Sew 3 pieced sashing units together, alternating with 2 setting cornerstones, to make 1 sashing row. Press. Repeat to make 3 sashing rows total.

4. Sew the sampler blocks together into 4 rows of 3 blocks each, separated by pieced sashing units.

5. Sew the sampler block rows and sashing rows together, pressing after each addition.

6. Make the outer sashing:

   A. Using 14 gold 5¼″ triangles and the remaining 1¼″ cream strips, follow the instructions in Step 2A to make 14 gold/cream triangle units.

   B. Sew 2 dark green 3⅞″ triangles to each of the gold/cream triangle units created in Step 6A. Make 14 units.

   C. Sew 4 of the units created in Step 6B, alternating with 3 dark green 3½″ × 12½″ rectangles, into a strip. Sew 1 dark green 3½″ × 3½″ square to each end. Press. Repeat to make a second side outer sashing.

D. Sew 3 units created in Step 6B, alternating with 2 dark green 3½″ × 12½″ rectangles, into a strip. Sew 1 dark green 3½″ × 6½″ rectangle to each end to make the top outer sashing. Press. Repeat to make the bottom outer sashing.

E. Sew the side outer sashing to the sides of the quilt. Press. Sew the top and bottom sashing to the top and bottom of the quilt. Press.

7. Add butted borders. Sew 4 gold 3½″ strips together in pairs end to end to make 2 borders. Sew to the sides of the quilt and trim to fit. Press toward the gold fabric.

8. Cut 1 of the 3½″ gold strips in half. Sew the half-strips to the long strips in pairs end to end to make 2 borders. Sew to the top and bottom of the quilt. Press toward the gold fabric. Trim the excess.

9. Sew 4 dark rust 6½″ strips together in pairs end to end to make 2 borders. Sew to the sides of the quilt and trim to fit. Press toward the dark rust fabric.

10. Sew 4 dark rust 6½″ strips together in pairs end to end to make 2 borders. Sew to the top and bottom of the quilt and trim to fit. Press toward the dark rust fabric.

11. Layer the quilt top, batting, and backing. Baste. Quilt as desired. Attach a hanging sleeve, if desired, and bind with the dark rust fabric.

Quilt Assembly Diagram

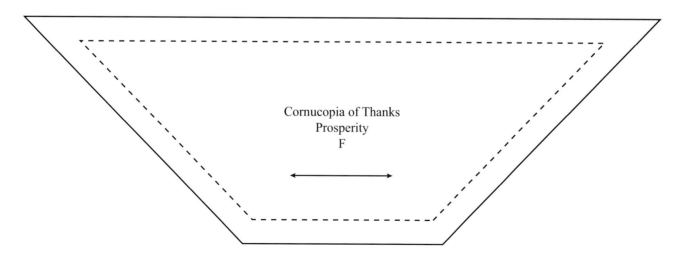

Cornucopia of Thanks
Prosperity
F

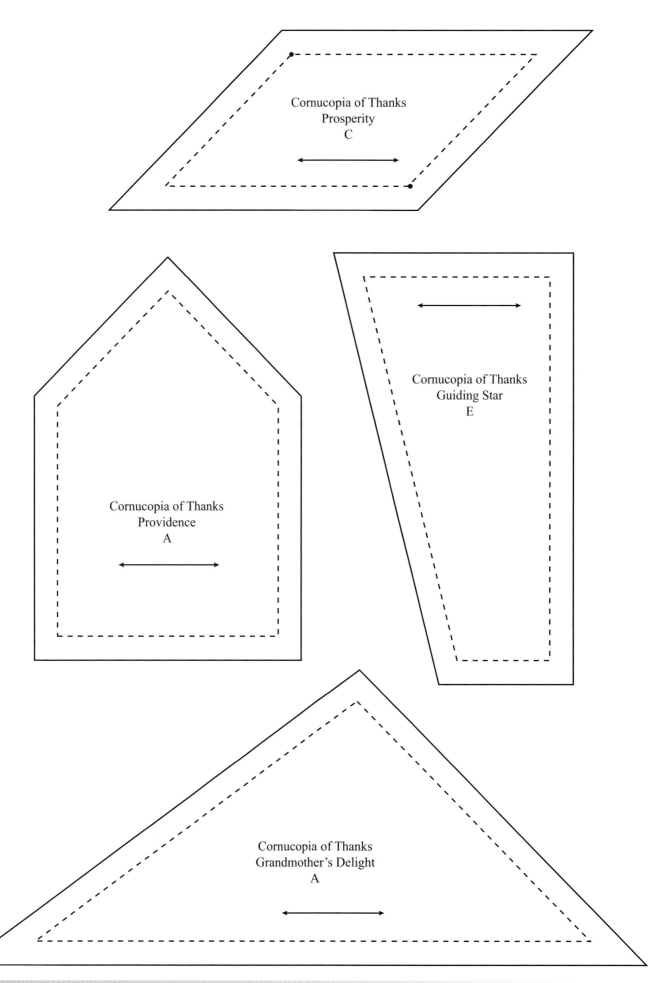

Cornucopia of Thanks
Prosperity
C

Cornucopia of Thanks
Guiding Star
E

Cornucopia of Thanks
Providence
A

Cornucopia of Thanks
Grandmother's Delight
A

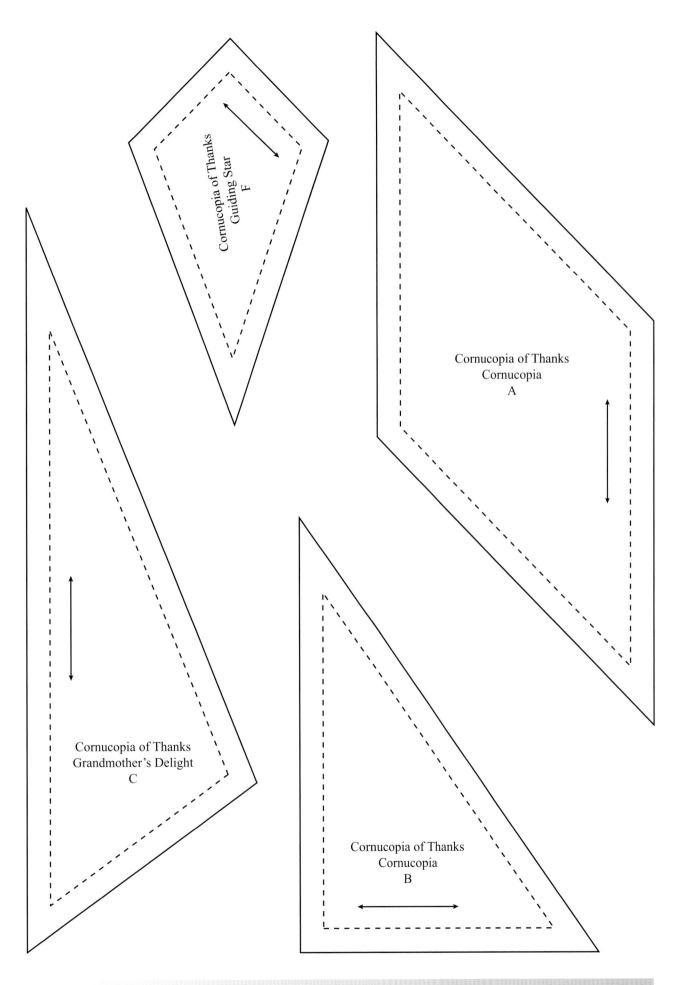

Cornucopia of Thanks
Guiding Star
F

Cornucopia of Thanks
Cornucopia
A

Cornucopia of Thanks
Grandmother's Delight
C

Cornucopia of Thanks
Cornucopia
B

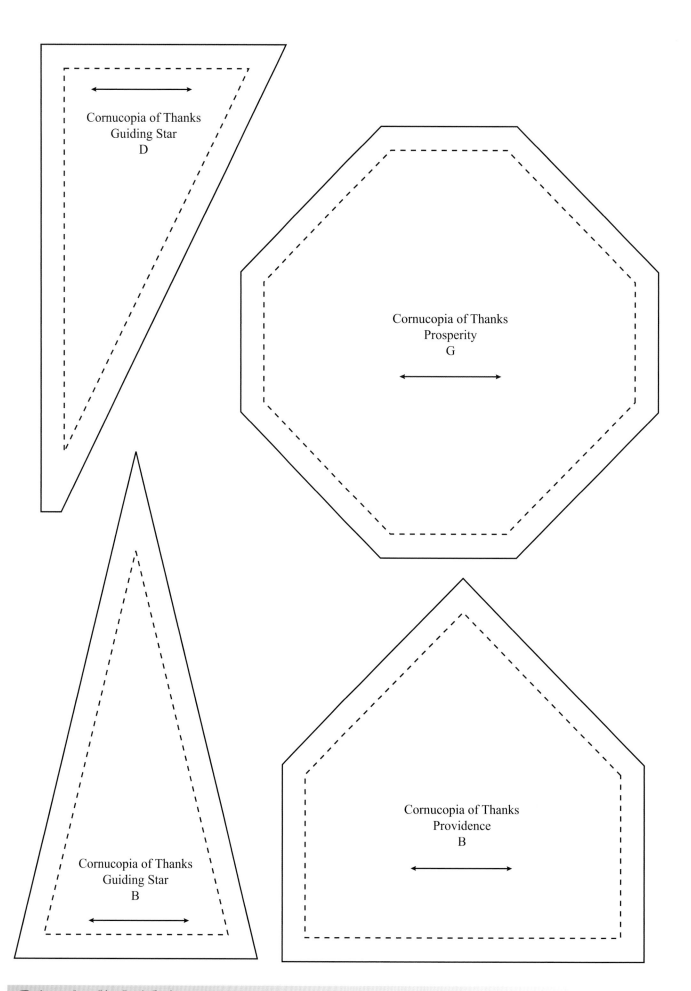

Cornucopia of Thanks
Guiding Star
D

Cornucopia of Thanks
Prosperity
G

Cornucopia of Thanks
Guiding Star
B

Cornucopia of Thanks
Providence
B

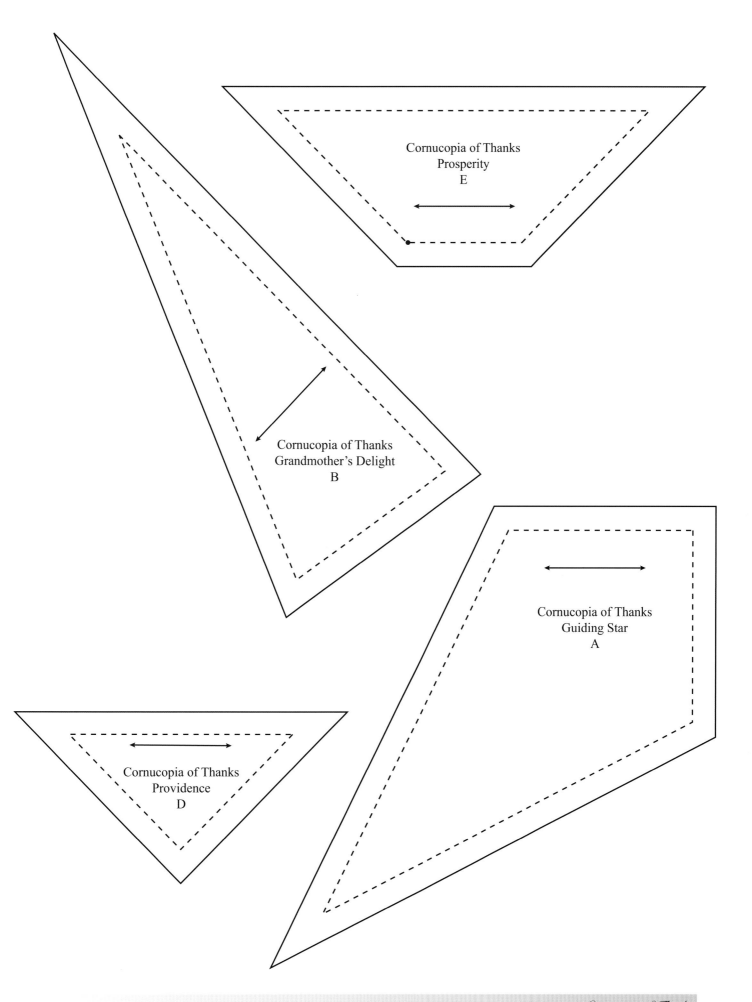

Cornucopia of Thanks
Prosperity
E

Cornucopia of Thanks
Grandmother's Delight
B

Cornucopia of Thanks
Guiding Star
A

Cornucopia of Thanks
Providence
D

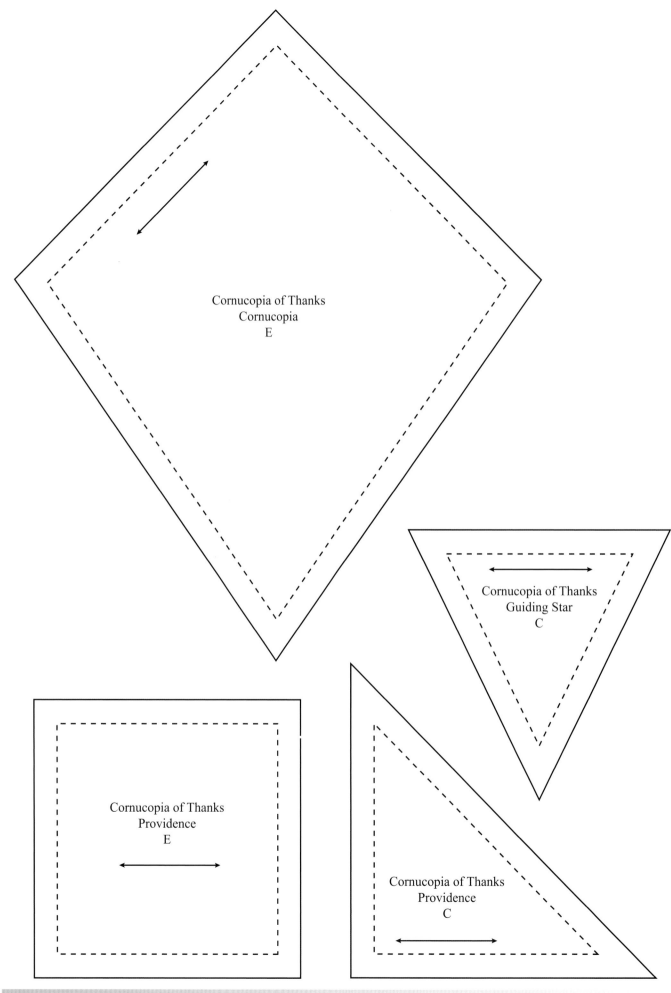

Cornucopia of Thanks
Cornucopia
E

Cornucopia of Thanks
Guiding Star
C

Cornucopia of Thanks
Providence
E

Cornucopia of Thanks
Providence
C

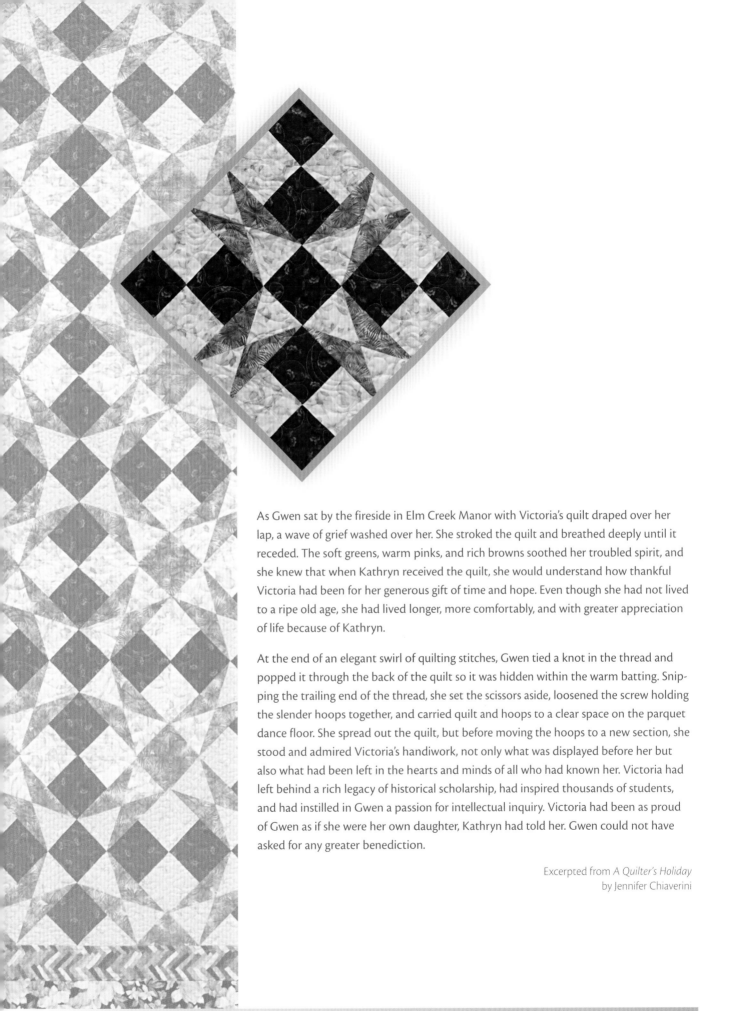

As Gwen sat by the fireside in Elm Creek Manor with Victoria's quilt draped over her lap, a wave of grief washed over her. She stroked the quilt and breathed deeply until it receded. The soft greens, warm pinks, and rich browns soothed her troubled spirit, and she knew that when Kathryn received the quilt, she would understand how thankful Victoria had been for her generous gift of time and hope. Even though she had not lived to a ripe old age, she had lived longer, more comfortably, and with greater appreciation of life because of Kathryn.

At the end of an elegant swirl of quilting stitches, Gwen tied a knot in the thread and popped it through the back of the quilt so it was hidden within the warm batting. Snipping the trailing end of the thread, she set the scissors aside, loosened the screw holding the slender hoops together, and carried quilt and hoops to a clear space on the parquet dance floor. She spread out the quilt, but before moving the hoops to a new section, she stood and admired Victoria's handiwork, not only what was displayed before her but also what had been left in the hearts and minds of all who had known her. Victoria had left behind a rich legacy of historical scholarship, had inspired thousands of students, and had instilled in Gwen a passion for intellectual inquiry. Victoria had been as proud of Gwen as if she were her own daughter, Kathryn had told her. Gwen could not have asked for any greater benediction.

Excerpted from *A Quilter's Holiday*
by Jennifer Chiaverini

Remembering Victoria

From *A Quilter's Holiday* by Jennifer Chiaverini

Designed and pieced by Jennifer Chiaverini, machine quilted by Sue Vollbrecht, 2009.

Finished Block: 12″ × 12″

Finished Quilt: 76″ × 76″

Number of Blocks: 25 Augusta blocks

Materials

Medium green: 1⅞ yards

Medium brown: 1⅜ yards

Cream: 1⅔ yards

Pink: 1¼ yards

Multicolored braid print or stripe: ¾ yard if the border is cut crosswise and pieced OR 1¼ yards if cut lengthwise and pieced

Floral print: 2¼ yards (includes ⅝ yard for the binding)

Backing: 5 yards

Batting: 84″ × 84″

Cutting Instructions

Copy Augusta template patterns A, B, and C on page 63 onto template material.

From Medium Green

- Cut 200 B triangles.
- Cut 50 squares 2⅞″ × 2⅞″. Cut each square in half diagonally once to make 100 E triangles.

From Medium Brown

- Cut 125 C squares.

From Cream

- Cut 128 A triangles.
- Cut 30 squares 5¼″ × 5¼″. Cut each square in half diagonally twice to make 120 D triangles.

From Pink

- Cut 72 A triangles.
- Cut 20 squares 5¼″ × 5¼″. Cut each square in half diagonally twice to make 80 D triangles.

From Multicolored Braid or Stripe

- Cut 8 strips 2½″ × width of fabric. (If cutting lengthwise, cut 8 strips 2½″ × length of fabric.) Pair the strips and sew them end to end to make 4 long strips (set aside for the inner borders).

From Floral Print

- Cut 8 strips 6½″ × width of fabric. Pair the strips and sew them end to end to make 4 long strips (set aside for the outer borders).

Block Assembly

1. Sew each A triangle to a B triangle. Press toward the green fabric.

2. Sew the A/B triangle units together in pairs, making 48 cream/cream pairs, 20 pink/pink pairs, and 32 cream/pink pairs.

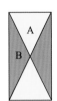

Make 48.   Make 20.   Make 32.

3. Sew 2 cream/cream pairs to opposite sides of a brown C square. Sew 2 green E triangles to opposite ends. Press. Repeat to make 8 center rows.

Make 8.

4. Sew 2 pink/pink pairs to opposite sides of a brown C square. Sew 2 green E triangles to opposite ends. Press. Repeat to make 5 center rows.

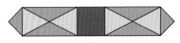

Make 5.

5. Sew 1 cream/cream pair and 1 cream/pink pair to opposite sides of a brown C square, placing the cream triangles adjacent to the brown square. Sew 2 green E triangles to opposite ends. Press. Repeat to make 8 center rows.

Make 8.

6. Sew 2 cream/pink pairs to opposite sides of a brown C square, placing the cream triangles adjacent to the brown square. Sew 2 green E triangles to opposite ends. Press. Repeat to make 4 center rows.

Make 4.

7. Sew 2 cream D triangles to adjacent sides of a brown C square. Press. Repeat to make 60 units. Sew 2 pink D triangles to adjacent sides of a brown C square. Press. Repeat to make 40 units.

Make 60.

Make 40.

8. Sew 2 of the brown/cream triangles created in the previous step to opposite sides of a cream/cream unit created in Step 2. Press. Sew a green E triangle to the corner. Press. Repeat to make 24 block rows.

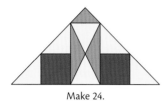

Make 24.

9. Sew 2 of the brown/pink triangles created in Step 7 to opposite sides of a pink/pink unit created in Step 2. Press. Sew a green E triangle to the corner. Press. Repeat to make 10 block rows.

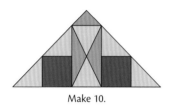

Make 10.

10. Sew 2 of the brown/pink triangles created in Step 7 to opposite sides of a cream/pink unit created in Step 2 as shown. Press. Sew a green E triangle to the corner. Press. Repeat to make 4 block rows.

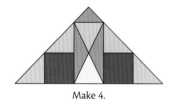

Make 4.

11. Sew 1 of the brown/cream triangles and 1 of the brown/pink triangles created in Step 7 to opposite sides of a cream/pink unit created in Step 2 as shown. Press. Sew a green E triangle to the corner. Press. Repeat to make 8 block rows and 4 mirror-image block rows.

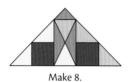

Make 8.

Make 4.

12. Following the block assembly diagrams for proper fabric placement, sew the top, center, and bottom rows together to make 25 Augusta blocks. Press.

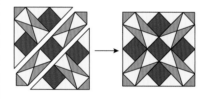

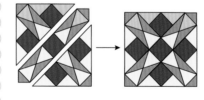

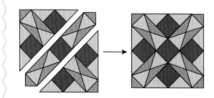

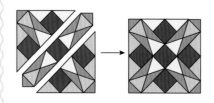

Quilt Construction

1. Sew the Augusta blocks into 5 rows of 5 blocks each, following the Quilt Assembly Diagram for correct block placement. Press.

2. Sew the rows together, pressing after each addition.

3. Sew each pieced inner border strip to a pieced outer border strip along the long edges. Press toward the floral print.

4. Center and sew 2 borders to the sides of the quilt, taking care not to sew into the ¼" seam allowance at the beginning and end. Press. Sew the remaining 2 borders to the top and bottom of the quilt, taking care not to sew into the ¼" seam allowance at the beginning and end. Press.

5. Miter the borders. (See Quiltmaking Basics, page 91.) Press.

6. Layer the quilt top, batting, and backing. Baste. Quilt as desired. Attach a hanging sleeve, if desired, and bind with the floral print.

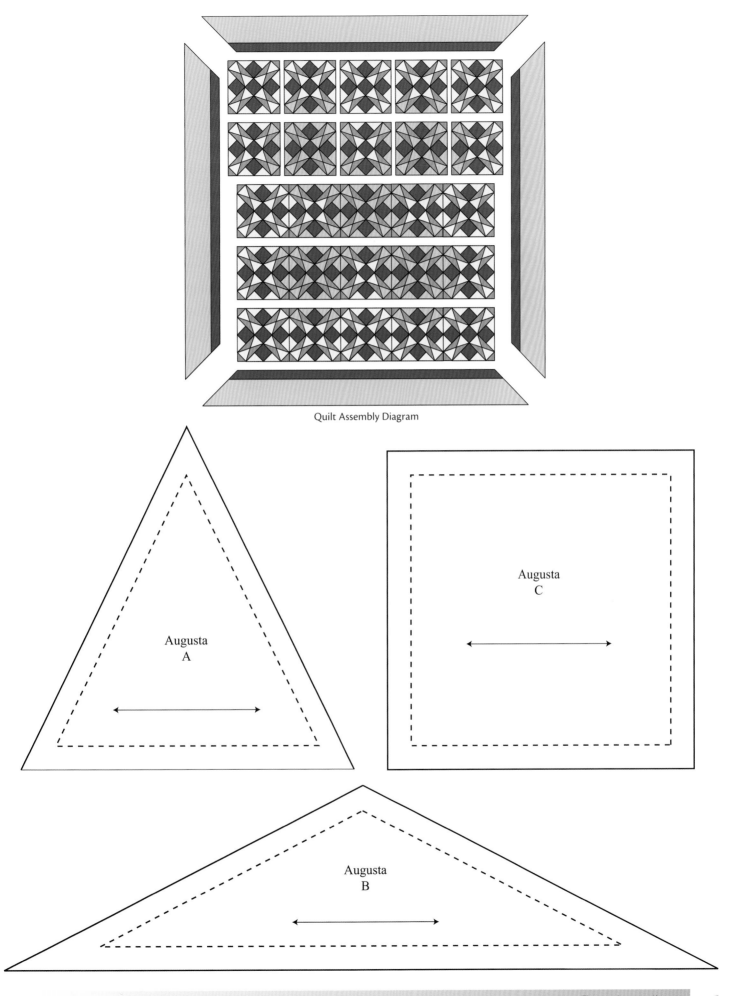

Quilt Assembly Diagram

Augusta
A

Augusta
C

Augusta
B

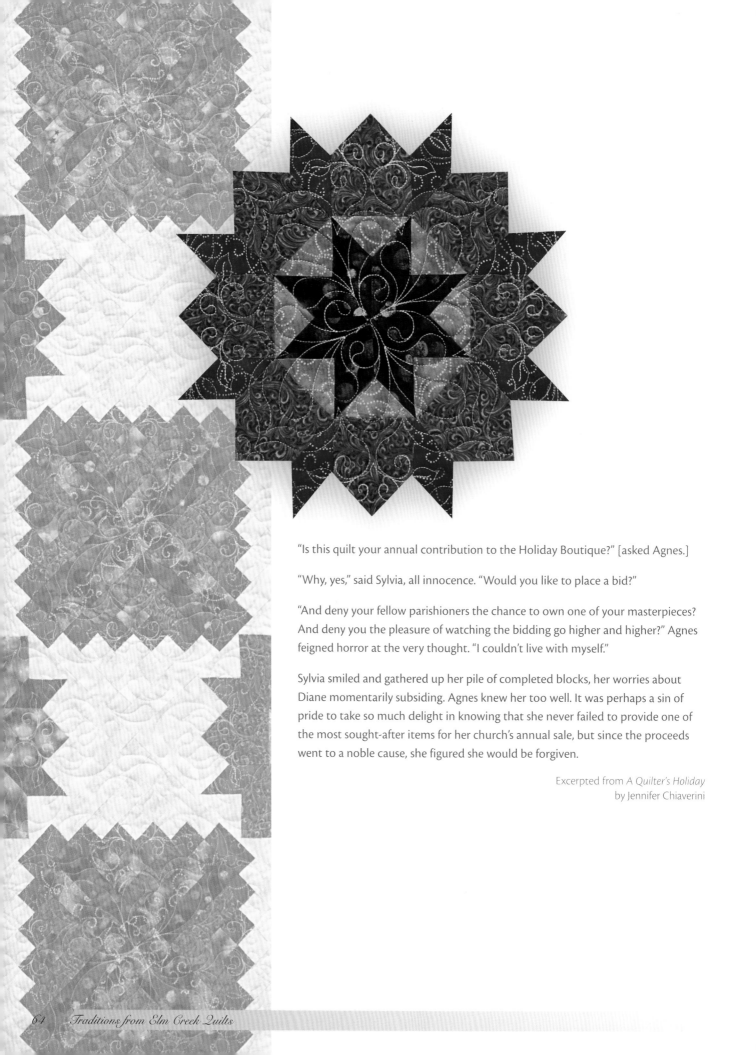

"Is this quilt your annual contribution to the Holiday Boutique?" [asked Agnes.]

"Why, yes," said Sylvia, all innocence. "Would you like to place a bid?"

"And deny your fellow parishioners the chance to own one of your masterpieces? And deny you the pleasure of watching the bidding go higher and higher?" Agnes feigned horror at the very thought. "I couldn't live with myself."

Sylvia smiled and gathered up her pile of completed blocks, her worries about Diane momentarily subsiding. Agnes knew her too well. It was perhaps a sin of pride to take so much delight in knowing that she never failed to provide one of the most sought-after items for her church's annual sale, but since the proceeds went to a noble cause, she figured she would be forgiven.

Excerpted from *A Quilter's Holiday*
by Jennifer Chiaverini

Holiday Blessings

From *A Quilter's Holiday* by Jennifer Chiaverini

Designed and pieced by Jennifer Chiaverini, machine quilted by Sue Vollbrecht, 2010.

Finished Block: Star of the Magi 12″ × 12″, Chimneys and Cornerstones 6″ × 6″
Finished Quilt: 67″ × 84″
Number of Blocks: 12 Star of the Magi blocks, 34 Chimneys and Cornerstones blocks

Materials

- Assorted reds: 2 yards total (includes the inner border)
- Assorted purples: 3 yards total (includes the outer border and binding)
- Assorted greens: 2 yards total
- Assorted golds: ⅔ yard total
- Golden beige: 2⅜ yards
- Batting: 75″ × 92″
- Backing: 5½ yards

Star of the Magi Cutting Instructions

Make templates by copying patterns A, B, and C on page 70 onto template material. Transfer all the dots from the templates onto the fabric pieces.

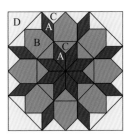

From Assorted Reds

- Cut 96 A diamonds.

From Assorted Purples

- Cut 96 A diamonds.

From Assorted Greens

- Cut 96 B pieces.

From Assorted Golds

- Cut 96 C triangles.

From Golden Beige

- Cut 192 C triangles.
- Cut 3 strips 4⅜″ × width of fabric; subcut into 24 squares 4⅜″ × 4⅜″. Cut each square in half diagonally once to make 48 D triangles.

Star of the Magi Block Assembly

Note: Consult a general quiltmaking book if you are unfamiliar with Y-seam construction.

1. Sewing only from dot to dot and not into the seam allowances, sew the purple diamonds (A) together in pairs. Backstitch at each end. Make 48.

2. Using Y-seam construction, set a gold triangle (C) into the angle between the A diamonds. Sewing only from dot to dot and backstitching at each end, attach another gold triangle (C) to the purple A diamond on the right. Make 48.

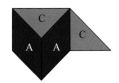

3. Using Y-seam construction and sewing only from dot to dot and backstitching at each end, join the units created in Step 2 into pairs. Make 24.

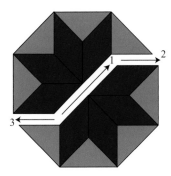

4. Sewing only from dot to dot, join the units created in Step 3 into pairs to make the central octagons. Make 12.

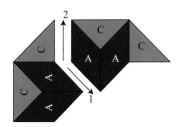

5. Sewing only from dot to dot, join 4 green pentagons (B) to opposite sides of the central octagon. Make 12 units.

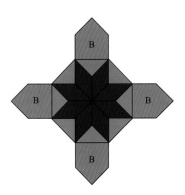

6. Sewing only from dot to dot, sew 2 red diamonds (A) to opposite sides of each remaining green pentagon (B). Using Y-seam construction, attach 2 golden beige triangles (C) to each unit. Make 48.

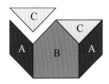

7. Using Y-seam construction and sewing only from dot to dot, attach 4 units created in Step 6 to a central octagon. First, sew the base of the green pentagon (B) to a gold triangle, and then sew the red diamonds to the adjacent green pentagons attached in Step 5. Repeat for the remaining 11 central octagons.

8. Using Y-seam construction, set small golden beige triangles (C) into the angles created between the green pentagons (B) and the red diamonds (A). Repeat for the remaining 11 blocks.

9. Sew the large golden beige triangles (D) to the 4 corners of each block. Make 12 Star of the Magi blocks.

Chimneys and Cornerstones Cutting Instructions

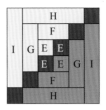

From Assorted Reds

- Cut 9 strips 1½" × width of fabric. Cut 3 of the strips in half to make 6 half-strips 1½" × 21".

From Assorted Greens

- Cut 2 strips 1½" × width of fabric. Cut 1 of the strips in half to make 2 half-strips 1½" × 21" (you will use only 1).

- Cut 2 strips 5½" × width of fabric (I). Cut 1 of the strips in half to make 2 I half-strips (you will use only 1).

- Cut 1 strip 4½" × width of fabric. Trim the width of 1 I half-strip (from above) to 4½". Subcut the strips into 34 rectangles 1½" × 4½" (H).

- Cut 2 strips 3½" × width of fabric (G). Cut 1 strip in half to make 2 G half-strips.

- Cut 1 strip 2½" × width of fabric. Trim the width of 1 G half-strip (from above) to 2½". Subcut the strips into 34 rectangles 1½" × 2½" (F).

From Golden Beige

- Cut 2 strips 1½" × width of fabric. Cut 1 of the strips in half to make 2 half-strips 1½" × 21" (you will use only 1).

- Cut 2 strips 5½" × width of fabric (I). Cut 1 of the strips in half to make 2 I half-strips (you will use only 1).

- Cut 1 strip 4½" × width of fabric. Trim the width of 1 I half-strip (from above) to 4½". Subcut the strips into 34 rectangles 1½" × 4½" (H).

- Cut 2 strips 3½" × width of fabric (G). Cut 1 of the strips in half to make 2 G half-strips (you will use only 1).

- Cut 1 strip 2½" × width of fabric. Trim the width of 1 G half-strip (from above) to 2½". Subcut the strips into 34 rectangles 1½" × 2½" (F).

Chimneys and Cornerstones Block Assembly

1. Sew the long side of a 1½″ red strip to the long side of a 1½″ green strip to make a strip set. Sew a 1½″ red half-strip to the 1½″ green half-strip to make a strip set. Press toward the red fabric. Subcut the strip sets into 34 red/green square units 1½″ × 2½″ (E/E).

2. Sew the long side of a 1½″ red strip to the long side of a golden beige strip to make a strip set. Sew a 1½″ red half-strip to the 1½″ golden beige half-strip to make a strip set. Press toward the red fabric. Subcut the strip sets into 34 red/golden beige square units 1½″ × 2½″ (E/E).

3. Nesting the seams, sew a red/green square unit to a red/golden beige square unit to make a four-patch. Press the seam open. Repeat to make 34.

4. Sew a 1½″ red strip to a 3½″ green strip. Sew a 1½″ red half-strip to a 3½″ green half-strip. Press toward the red fabric. Subcut the strip sets into 34 green/red units 1½″ × 4½″ (G).

5. Sew a 1½″ red strip to a 3½″ golden beige strip. Sew a 1½″ red half-strip to the 3½″ golden beige half-strip. Press toward the red fabric. Subcut the strip sets into 34 golden beige/red units 1½″ × 4½″ (G).

6. Sew a 1½″ red strip to a 5½″ green strip. Sew a 1½″ red half-strip to the 5½″ green half-strip. Press toward the red fabric. Subcut the strip sets into 34 green/red units 1½″ × 6½″ (I).

7. Sew a 1½″ red strip to a 5½″ golden beige strip. Sew a 1½″ red half-strip to the 5½″ golden beige half-strip. Press toward the red fabric. Subcut the strip sets to make 34 golden beige/red units 1½″ × 6½″ (I).

8. Sew 1 golden beige F rectangle and 1 green F rectangle to opposite sides of a central four-patch. Press. Repeat to make 34.

9. Sew 1 golden beige/red G unit and 1 green/red G unit to opposite sides of a central four-patch unit, perpendicular to the E rectangle seams. Press. Repeat to make 34.

10. Sew 1 golden beige H rectangle and 1 green H rectangle to opposite sides of the blocks. Press. Make 34.

11. Sew 1 golden beige/red I unit and 1 green/red I unit to opposite sides of each block. Press. Make 34 Chimneys and Cornerstones blocks.

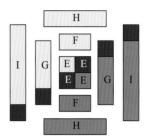

Setting Triangle and Border Cutting Instructions

From Golden Beige

- Cut 5 squares 7¼″ × 7¼″. Cut each square in half diagonally twice to make 20 setting triangles (J).

- Cut 2 squares 9⅜″ × 9⅜″. Cut each square in half diagonally once to make 4 corner setting triangles (K).

Note: To help prevent the bias edges from stretching, spray the fabric with sizing and press with hot iron before cutting.

From Red

- Cut 10 strips 2½″ × width of fabric. Cut 1 of the strips in half to make 2 half-strips 2½″ × 21″.

From Purple

- Cut 10 strips 6½″ × width of fabric. Cut 1 of the strips in half to make 2 half-strips 6½″ × 21″.

Quilt Assembly

Note: If you are unfamiliar with mitering borders, see Quiltmaking Basics, page 91.

1. Sew 2 Chimneys and Cornerstones blocks together, green sides together. Press. Repeat to make a second pair. Press. Nesting the seams, sew the pairs together. Press. Repeat to make 6.

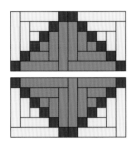

2. Sew 2 J triangles to the green sides of the remaining Chimneys and Cornerstones blocks. Press. Make 10 Chimneys and Cornerstones setting triangles.

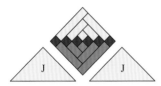

3. Following the Quilt Assembly Diagram, sew the Star of the Magi blocks, Chimneys and Cornerstones block units, Chimneys and Cornerstones / triangles units, and K triangles into diagonal rows. Press.

4. Sew the rows together, pressing after each addition.

5. Sew 2 red strips and 1 red half-strip together end to end. Press. Repeat to make a second long red strip.

6. Sew 2 purple strips and 1 purple half-strip together end to end. Press. Repeat to make a second long purple strip.

7. Sew 1 long red strip to 1 long purple strip along the long edges to make a long border. Press. Repeat to make a second long border.

8. Sew the long borders to the sides of the quilt, taking care not to sew into the ¼" seam allowance at the corners of the K triangles.

9. Sew 2 red strips together end to end. Press. Repeat to make a second short red strip.

10. Sew 2 purple strips together end to end. Press. Repeat to make a second short purple strip.

11. Sew 1 short red strip to 1 short purple strip to make a top border. Press. Repeat to make a bottom border.

12. Sew the short borders to the top and bottom of the quilt, stopping and backstitching ¼" in from each corner.

13. Miter the borders. Press.

14. Layer the quilt top, batting, and backing. Baste. Quilt as desired. Attach a hanging sleeve, if desired, and bind with purple fabric.

Quilt Assembly Diagram

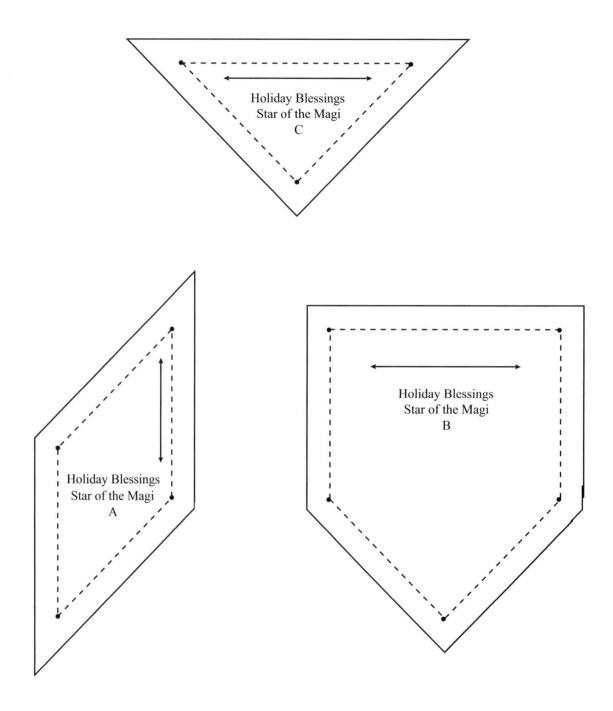

Holiday Blessings
Star of the Magi
C

Holiday Blessings
Star of the Magi
A

Holiday Blessings
Star of the Magi
B

FROM
The Aloha Quilt

Another season of Elm Creek Quilt Camp has come to a close, and Bonnie Markham faces a bleak and lonely winter ahead with her quilt shop out of business and her divorce looming. A welcome escape comes when Claire, a dear college friend, unexpectedly invites her to Maui to help launch an exciting new business: a quilters' retreat set at a bed-and-breakfast amid the vibrant colors and balmy breezes of the Hawaiian Islands. Soon Bonnie finds herself looking out upon sparkling waters and banyan trees, helping to run Claire's inn, planning quilting courses, and learning the history and intricacies of Hawaiian quilting.

Bonnie's mentor in the art of Hawaiian quilting, Midori Tanaka, encourages her to create her own original pattern so that her first quilt in the Hawaiian style will be uniquely hers. Inspired by the pineapples growing in the garden of the Hale Kapa Kuiki, Claire's bed-and-breakfast in Lahaina, Bonnie designs *Pineapple Patch* after viewing several works in progress at a meeting of Midori's quilting bee, the Laulima Quilters.

The Aloha Quilt of the title doesn't appear until the end of the story. Another new friend, Hinano Paoa, designs the pattern for Bonnie as a farewell gift upon her departure from Maui. His nickname for Bonnie is Snowbird, because she has come to Hawaii only for the winter, and he fittingly chooses the bird of paradise flower for his design.

The fabrics for both quilts come from my Red Rooster fabric line Elm Creek Quilts: The Aloha Quilt Collection.

For her first quilt in the Hawaiian style, Bonnie decided to draw upon the natural beauties of the islands as well as a traditional symbol of welcome: the pineapple. The foundation paper pieced Pineapple block was one of her favorites, making this new interpretation of the theme even more appropriate and meaningful.

She cut a piece of paper one yard square, and then folded it into eighths as Midori had shown her. Studying the pineapples growing in the lanai garden, sketching, erasing, trying again, Bonnie drew a plump, ripe pineapple crowned with short, spiky leaves, set snugly within a flourish of long, slender, tapering fronds. She tried to imagine how her pattern would look after she cut it out and unfolded it, and when she thought she had it just about right, she carried her supplies upstairs to her suite and held the edge of the folded paper up to her bathroom mirror. The reflected image gave her a better idea of what the whole pattern would look like when complete and she was inspired to make a few changes—an erasure here, a smoother curve there—until at last she was pleased with what she saw.

It was time to commit herself, to put scissors to paper and see if what she had created matched what she had envisioned.

Excerpted from *The Aloha Quilt* by Jennifer Chiaverini

Pineapple Patch

From *The Aloha Quilt* by Jennifer Chiaverini

Designed and appliquéd by Jennifer Chiaverini, machine quilted by Sue Vollbrecht, 2010.

Finished Quilt: 54″ × 54″

Materials

Ivory solid or tone-on-tone fabric: 2¾ yards

Emerald green solid or tone-on-tone fabric: 2¾ yards

Backing: 3¼ yards

Batting: 62″ × 62″

Cutting Instructions

From Ivory Solid or Tone-on-Tone Fabric

● Cut 1 strip 58″ × width of fabric. Remove the selvages.

● Cut 2 strips 16″ × width of fabric. Remove the selvages.

Emerald Green Solid or Tone-on-Tone Fabric

● Cut 1 strip 56″ × width of fabric. Remove the selvages.

● Cut 2 strips 14″ × width of fabric. Remove the selvages.

Top Assembly

1. Sew the 16″-wide ivory strips together end to end. Press the seam open.

2. Sew the long edge of the strip created in the previous step to the long edge of the 58″-long ivory strip. Press the seam open.

3. Trim the ivory fabric to a 58″ × 58″ square.

4. Carefully and accurately fold the ivory square in half once horizontally, once vertically, and once along the diagonal. Press, creasing the folds to mark appliqué placement lines. Set aside.

Fold 1

Fold 2

Fold 3

5. Sew the 14″-wide emerald green strips together end to end. Press the seam open.

6. Sew the long edge of the strip created in Step 5 to the long edge of the 56″-long emerald green strip. Press the seam open.

7. Trim the emerald green fabric to a 54″ × 54″ square.

8. Carefully and accurately fold the emerald green square in half once horizontally, once vertically, and once along the diagonal as you did with the ivory square. Press, creasing the folds. Baste the emerald green triangle along all 3 sides and down the center, adding more basting stitches as needed to keep the folds flat and secure.

9. Make a template by connecting the 2 sections of the *Pineapple Patch* template pattern (pullout page P4) as indicated on the pattern. Place the template on the emerald green folded triangle, taking care to align the edges and keep the correct distance between the center (the *piko*) and the border (the *lei*). Trace around the template.

10. Carefully cut out the appliqué center and lei, adding a ⅛″ seam allowance around the appliqué design. Note: It can be difficult to cut through 8 layers of fabric, so be sure to use sharp cutting tools. Take care to keep the folds secure. Pin if necessary if you cut through basting stitches.

11. Unfold the ivory square on a flat surface, right side up. Carefully unfold the emerald green appliqué pieces and place them right side up on the ivory square, using the ironed horizontal, vertical, and diagonal creases to center the appliqué pieces.

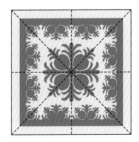

12. Ease the appliqués into place and pin them to the ivory square. Baste ¼" inside the edges of the appliqués. Remove the pins.

13. Using the ¼" basting stitches as a guide, turn the edge of the fabric under until it meets the stitches. Appliqué the emerald green pieces to the ivory background, using the tip of your needle to turn under the fabric edge just ahead of your stitching.

14. Trim away the excess ivory background fabric, squaring up the quilt top if necessary.

15. Remove the basting stitches and press.

Quilt Construction

Layer the quilt top, batting, and backing. Baste. Hawaiian quilts traditionally use echo quilting and additional quilting stitches to add details such as stems and leaves, but you should quilt as inspired. Attach a hanging sleeve, if desired, and bind with the emerald green fabric.

Quilt Assembly Diagram

Only months before [Bonnie] had thought she had lost everything, but she had emerged with a new business partnership, new friends, a new understanding and respect for Claire—and new love. And a new quilt to look forward to creating, from choosing the fabric to cutting out the appliqué to reminiscing about her Hawaiian adventure as she took one careful stitch after another. She remembered what Midori had told her so many weeks before, that all true Hawaiian quilt patterns were unique, made for a particular person, purpose, or occasion. "An original quilt pattern is a precious gift and a sign of great friendship," Midori had said, "because of the prayers and good wishes—part of the very spirit of the designer—that go into its creation."

She knew this was true of the quilt Hinano had designed for her, and that, perhaps without realizing it, he had captured the meaning and purpose of her journey and all the blessings it had bestowed upon her in every bird of paradise blossom he had drawn, in every graceful curve and elegant point of his pattern. She knew then that she would always think of it as the Aloha Quilt, for it conveyed the spirit of aloha as beautifully and perfectly as any creation of human hands ever could.

Excerpted from *The Aloha Quilt*
by Jennifer Chiaverini

The Aloha Quilt

From *The Aloha Quilt* by Jennifer Chiaverini

Designed and appliquéd by Jennifer Chiaverini, machine quilted by Sue Vollbrecht, 2010.

Finished Quilt: 54" × 54"

Materials

Ivory solid or tone-on-tone fabric: 2¾ yards

Red solid or tone-on-tone fabric: 2¾ yards

Backing: 3¼ yards

Batting: 62″ × 62″

Cutting Instructions

From Ivory Solid or Tone-on-Tone Fabric

- Cut 1 strip 58″ × width of fabric. Remove the selvages.
- Cut 2 strips 16″ × width of fabric. Remove the selvages.

Red Solid or Tone-on-Tone Fabric

- Cut 1 strip 56″ × width of fabric. Remove the selvages.
- Cut 2 strips 14″ × width of fabric. Remove the selvages.

Top Assembly

1. Sew the 16″-wide ivory strips together end to end. Press the seam open.

2. Sew the long edge of the strip created in Step 1 to the long edge of the 58″-long ivory strip. Press the seam open.

3. Trim the ivory fabric to a 58″ × 58″ square.

4. Carefully and accurately fold the ivory square in half once horizontally, once vertically, and once along the diagonal. Press, creasing the folds to mark appliqué placement lines. Set aside.

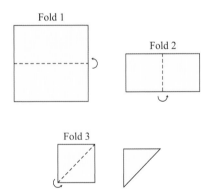

5. Sew the 14″-wide red strips together end to end. Press the seam open.

6. Sew the long edge of the strip created in the previous step to the long edge of the 56″-long red strip. Press the seam open.

7. Trim the red fabric to a 54″ × 54″ square.

8. Carefully and accurately fold the red square in half once horizontally, once vertically, and once along the diagonal. Press, creasing the folds. Baste the red triangle along all 3 sides and down the center, adding more basting stitches as needed to keep the folds flat and secure.

9. Make a template by connecting the 2 sections of *The Aloha Quilt* template pattern (pullout page P3) as indicated on the pattern. Place the template on the red folded triangle, taking care to align the edges and keep the correct distance between the center (the *piko*) and the border (the *lei*). Trace around the template.

10. Carefully cut out the appliqué center and lei, adding a ⅛″ seam allowance around the appliqué design. Note: It can be difficult to cut through 8 layers of fabric, so be sure to use sharp cutting tools. Take care to keep the folds secure. Pin if necessary if you cut through basting stitches.

11. Unfold the ivory square on a flat surface, right side up. Carefully unfold the red appliqué pieces and place them right side up on the ivory square, using the ironed horizontal, vertical, and diagonal creases to center the appliqué pieces.

12. Ease the appliqués into place and pin them to the ivory square. Baste ¼″ inside the edges of the appliqués. Remove the pins.

13. Using the ¼" basting stitches as a guide, turn the edge of the fabric under until it meets the stitches. Appliqué the red pieces to the ivory background, using the tip of your needle to turn under the fabric edge just ahead of your stitching.

14. Trim away the excess ivory background fabric, squaring up the quilt top if necessary.

15. Remove the basting stitches and press.

Quilt Construction

Layer the quilt top, batting, and backing. Baste. Hawaiian quilts traditionally use echo quilting, but you should quilt as inspired. Attach a hanging sleeve, if desired, and bind with the red fabric.

Quilt Assembly Diagram

FROM
The Union Quilters

In *The Union Quilters*, a remarkable group of women cope with changing roles and the extraordinary experiences of the Civil War. In 1862, when the men they love rally to answer Mr. Lincoln's call to arms, Gerda Bergstrom, Dorothea Nelson, and the other women of the Elm Creek Valley support one another through loneliness and fear. Letters from the front carry home the men's love and affection, but also their concern and frustration as the soldiers encounter not only mortal peril but also shortages of food, clothing, and medicine. With Dorothea leading the way, the women toil on the home front to provide the men of the 49th Pennsylvania and the 6th United States Colored Troops with necessary provisions, never suspecting that their newly acquired independence might forever alter the patchwork of town life in ways that transcend even the ultimate sacrifices of war.

When Dorothea's husband marches off to war, she urges him to take his favorite Dove in the Window quilt with him. This gentle reminder of his beloved wife offers Thomas warmth and comfort for many months, but he gives it away to a seriously wounded young Confederate soldier he rescues on the Gettysburg battlefield. My mother, Geraldine Neidenbach, pieced this version of *Dorothea's Dove in the Window* using fabrics in the Turkey red, Prussian blue, and light tan hues popular in the era.

At the foot of their bed [Dorothea] threw open the lid to the steamer trunk Uncle Jacob had bequeathed her and withdrew a quilt she had packed away for the summer. She draped it over the bed, sparing only a glance for the painstakingly arranged triangles and squares of Turkey red and Prussian blue and sun-bleached muslin, some scraps carefully saved from her household sewing, others shared by a dressmaker friend and others among her sewing circle. She folded the quilt in half lengthwise, quickly rolled it up into a tight bundle, and tied it off with a wide length of ribbon she had been saving for a hatband. When she returned outside, Thomas had the horses ready and waiting. He watched, silent and perplexed, as she placed the quilt into the back of the wagon with his pack and provisions.

"It's the Dove in the Window," she said, climbing onto the seat beside him as he gathered the reins. "I know it's your favorite."

"It's yours as well. I shouldn't take it."

"It's hardly my favorite. I prefer our wedding quilt and the Delectable Mountains I made for my uncle. But even if it were, I would rather you had it."

He shook his head. "It's too fine to take on the road. It could be soiled or torn or lost. Likely the army will issue us sturdy blankets with our uniforms."

"And if they don't, or if those blankets are delayed?" Dorothea countered. "You'll be grateful for this quilt when winter comes, even if you can't appreciate it now."

"I do appreciate it, all the more so because I recall how hard you worked on it. Think of the conditions we'll face—"

"I am thinking of the conditions you'll face." She felt wretched, helpless, but she fought to keep her voice even. "Take the quilt. It's not much to carry, and it'll comfort me to know that it's keeping you warm when I can't."

He fell silent, his eyes searching her face. "Very well." He chirruped to the horses. "You're right. If I don't take it, I'll regret it later."

Unwilling to trust herself to speak, she nodded and pressed herself against him on the wagon seat, heartsick, resting her head on his shoulder, imagining she could feel the warmth of his skin upon hers, his arms around her. She longed to lay her head on his chest, pull the quilt over them both, and sleep, sleep until the war passed over them like a thundercloud, holding the worst of its torrent until it cleared the mountains.

Excerpted from *The Union Quilters*
by Jennifer Chiaverini

Dorothea's Dove in the Window

From *The Union Quilters* by Jennifer Chiaverini

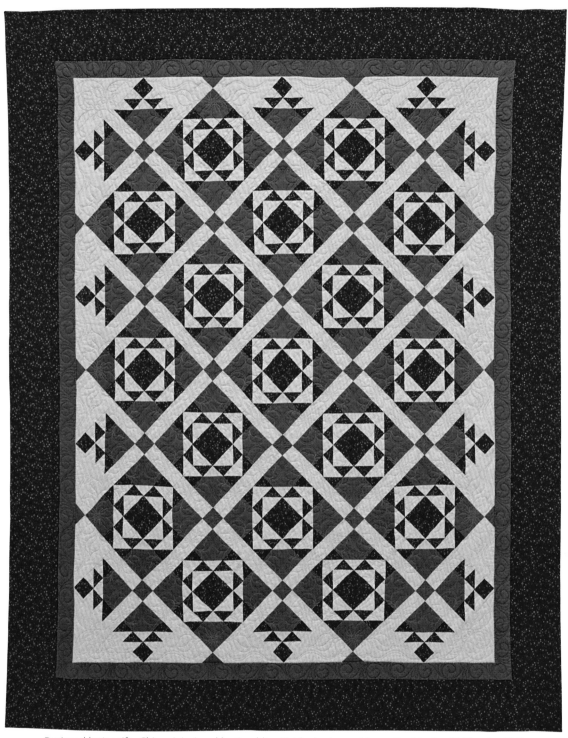

Designed by Jennifer Chiaverini, pieced by Geraldine Neidenbach, machine quilted by Sue Vollbrecht, 2010.

Finished Block: 12¼″ × 12¼″

Finished Quilt: 68″ × 85¼″

Number of Blocks: 18 blocks, 10 setting triangles

Materials

Turkey red: 3½ yards (includes the outer border and binding)

Prussian blue: 2 yards (includes the inner border)

Light beige: 3 yards

Backing: 5¼ yards

Batting: 76" × 94"

Cutting Instructions

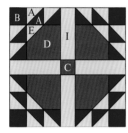

From Turkey Red

● Cut 11 strips 2⅝" × width of fabric; subcut into 164 squares 2⅝" × 2⅝" (A).

● Cut 5 strips 2¼" × width of fabric; subcut into 82 squares 2¼" × 2¼" (B).

● Cut 8 strips 6½" × width of fabric for the outer border.

From Prussian Blue

● Cut 1 strip 2¼" × width of fabric; subcut into 18 squares 2¼" × 2¼" (C).

● Cut 9 strips 4" × width of fabric; subcut into 82 squares 4" × 4" (D).

● Cut 3 squares 3¾" × 3¾". Cut each square in half diagonally twice to make 12 F triangles (you will use 10).

● Cut 9 strips 2½" × width of fabric for the inner border.

From Light Beige

● Cut 11 strips 2⅝" × width of fabric; subcut into 164 squares 2⅝" × 2⅝" (A).

● Cut 5 strips 2¼" × width of fabric; subcut into 82 squares 2¼" × 2¼" (E).

● Cut 6 strips 5¾" × width of fabric; subcut into 92 rectangles 2¼" × 5¾" (I).

Note: Before cutting triangles G and H, spray the fabric generously with sizing and press dry with a hot iron. This will help prevent the bias edges from stretching.

● Cut 5 squares 8¾" × 8¾". Cut each square in half diagonally twice to make 20 G triangles.

● Cut 2 squares 8" × 8". Cut the squares in half diagonally once to make 4 H setting triangles.

Block Assembly

1. Draw a dashed diagonal line from corner to corner on the wrong side of each 2¼" × 2¼" light beige E square. Draw a solid diagonal line ¼" from 1 side of the dashed line.

2. Pair a light beige E square with a Prussian blue D square, right sides facing and 1 corner and 2 sides matching. Sew on the dashed line. Trim excess fabric along the solid line and press toward the darker fabric. Repeat to make 82 E/D units.

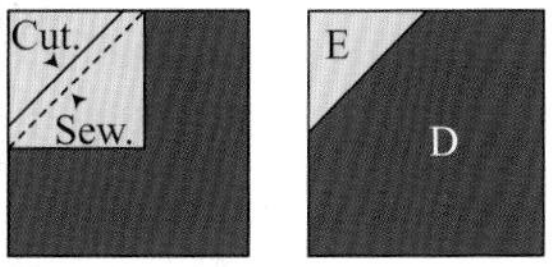

3. Make 328 quick-pieced triangle-squares:

A. Draw a solid diagonal line from corner to corner on the wrong side of a 2⅝" × 2⅝" light beige A square.

B. Pair each light beige A square with a Turkey red A square, right sides facing. Sew ¼" from each side of the drawn line. Cut on the solid line

to make 2 half-square triangle units. Press toward the darker fabric.

C. Repeat to make a total of 328 quick-pieced half-square triangle units.

4. Sew the triangle-squares into 82 pairs and 82 mirror-image pairs, following the diagram for fabric placement. Press.

Mirror-image half-square triangle pair

Half-square triangle pair

5. Sew a Turkey red B square to the end of a half-square triangle pair created in the previous step. Press. Repeat to make 82.

6. Sew a Turkey red mirror-image half-square triangle / square pair to a Prussian blue unit created in Step 2. Press. Attach a unit created in Step 5. Press. Repeat to create 82 corner units. Set aside 10 corner units for the setting triangles.

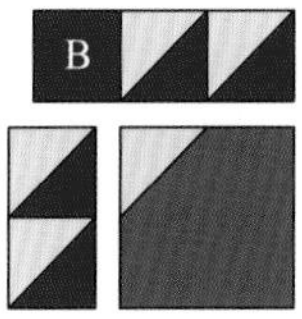

7. Sew 2 light beige I rectangles to opposite sides of a Prussian blue C square. Press. Repeat to make 18 center rows.

8. Sew 2 corner units to opposite sides of a light beige I rectangle. Press. Repeat to make 18 top and 18 bottom rows.

9. Sew a top, middle, and bottom row together to complete 1 block. Repeat to make a total of 18 Dove in the Window blocks.

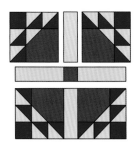

10. To complete the setting triangles, sew a light beige rectangle to each remaining corner unit. Press. Repeat to make 10 units.

11. Sew the short side of a Prussian blue triangle F to an end of each remaining beige I rectangle. Press. Repeat to make 10.

12. Pair each unit created in Step 11 with a unit created in Step 10. Sew and press. Make 10.

13. Sew 2 G triangles to a unit created in Step 12. Press. Repeat to make 10 setting triangles.

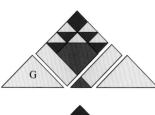

Quilt Construction

Note: If you are unfamiliar with mitering borders, see Quiltmaking Basics on page 91.

1. Sew the Dove in the Window blocks and pieced setting triangles into diagonal rows. Press.

2. Sew the rows together, pressing after each addition.

3. Attach the light beige H setting triangles to make the 4 corners. Press.

4. Sew the same-color border strips together, end to end, in pairs. Cut 1 of the red and 1 of the blue border strips in half and add a half-strip to 2 of the pairs for the side borders. Sew each pieced Prussian blue strip to a pieced Turkey red strip along the long edges. Press.

5. Center a border on each side of the quilt, pin, and sew, stopping and back-stitching ¼" inside the corner at the beginning and end of the seam. Press.

6. Repeat Step 5 and sew the shorter borders to the top and bottom of the quilt. Press. Miter the borders. Press.

7. Layer the quilt top, batting, and backing. Baste. Quilt as desired. Attach a hanging sleeve, if desired, and bind with the Turkey red fabric.

Quilt Assembly Diagram

FROM

The Wedding Quilt

The Wedding Quilt transports readers 25 years into the future to the wedding day of Sarah and Matt's daughter, Caroline. Elm Creek Manor has seen many changes since the snowy February day when the twins were born, but the friendship and love of the Elm Creek Quilters have endured.

Almost one hundred years earlier, the women of the Bergstrom family had made a beautiful Double Wedding Ring quilt embellished with floral appliqués for Sylvia's favorite cousin, Elizabeth Bergstrom Nelson. Elizabeth took the quilt with her when, soon after their marriage in 1925, she and her new husband moved to Southern California—where the quilt disappeared from family history. When Sylvia's search for the missing quilt proves unsuccessful, she re-creates the quilt from memory and sets it aside for her darling Caroline's wedding day. My own re-creation of *Caroline's Wedding* uses fabrics from Elm Creek Quilts: Elizabeth's Collection from Red Rooster Fabrics.

[Caroline] lifted the white cardboard lid, brushed aside layers of tissue paper, and gasped. "It's a quilt." She took the soft, folded bundle from the box and stood, and Sarah quickly stepped forward to help her unfold it.

Then Sarah, too, gasped as recognition struck her. Sylvia's gift was a Double Wedding Ring quilt in a gradation of pink and green hues, embellished with floral appliqués—the reproduction of the beautiful, long-lost quilt the women of the Bergstrom family had made for Sylvia's beloved cousin, Elizabeth.

The letter Sylvia included with the quilt explained everything ... "You may not remember this, my darling Caroline," Sylvia had written, "but when you were young, you often watched me as I worked upon this quilt, and I knew how much you admired it. One day you asked me, very sweetly, if I would please make a quilt just like it for you when you became a bride like Elizabeth. I told you I would try my very best to do so, but even then my fingers were failing me, and I soon realized that this would be my last quilt. And so it is, and so, my dear, it is yours. I hope your marriage is blessed with love and happiness, and when you and your new husband sleep beneath this quilt, I pray it brings you good, peaceful dreams."

Excerpted from *The Wedding Quilt*
by Jennifer Chiaverini

Caroline's Wedding

From *The Wedding Quilt* by Jennifer Chiaverini

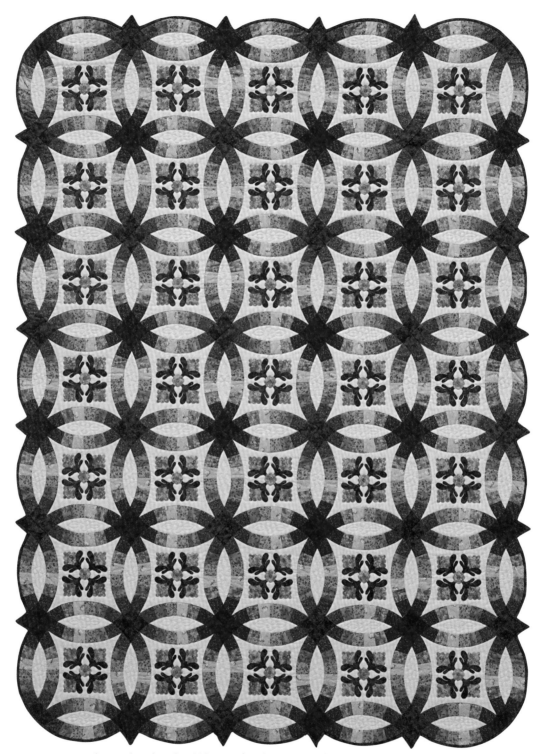

Designed, pieced, and appliquéd by Jennifer Chiaverini, machine quilted by Sue Vollbrecht, 2010.

Finished Block: approximately 15″ diameter
Finished Quilt: 57″ × 78″
Number of Blocks: 35 interlocking rings

Materials

Very dark red: ½ yard

Dark red: ¾ yard

Medium red: 1¼ yards

Medium-light red: ¾ yard

Very dark green: 1¼ yards

Dark green: ¾ yard

Medium green: ¾ yard

Medium-light green: ¾ yard

Gold: ⅛ yard

Brown: ⅛ yard or scrap

Cream: 4 yards

Backing: 5 yards

Fabric for double-fold bias binding: 1 yard

Batting: 65″ × 86″

Cutting Instructions

Copy template patterns A–E on pattern pullout page P2 onto template material. Transfer all the dots from the templates onto the fabric pieces.

Trace patterns F–I on pattern pullout page P2 and prepare according to your favorite appliqué method.

Note: To help prevent the bias edges from stretching, spray the fabric with sizing and iron before cutting the Double Wedding Ring pieces. To make cutting simpler and faster, use acrylic templates such as Sharlene Jorgenson's Quilting from the Heartland Double Wedding Ring templates. Adjust the size of the floral appliqué designs if necessary to fit.

From Very Dark Red

- Cut 92 C pieces.

From Dark Red

- Cut 82 B pieces. Flip over the template and cut 82 B Reverse pieces.

From Medium Red

- Cut 164 A pieces.
- Cut 140 flowers (F).

From Medium-Light Red

- Cut 164 A pieces.

From Very Dark Green

- Cut 92 C pieces.
- Cut 140 stems (G).

From Dark Green

- Cut 82 B pieces. Flip over the template and cut 82 B Reverse pieces.

From Medium Green

- Cut 164 A pieces.

From Medium-Light Green

- Cut 164 A pieces.

From Gold

- Cut 35 center flowers (H).

From Brown

- Cut 35 center circles (I). Note: If you prefer to use reverse appliqué, cut patches larger than template I. See Block Assembly Step 11.

From Cream

- Cut 82 D pieces.
- Cut 35 E pieces.

Block Assembly

1. Pair each medium green A with a medium-light green A. Sew 82 of the pairs together along a straight edge with the medium-light green piece on top. Make 82 mirror-image pairs by sewing the remaining pairs together with the medium green piece on top. Make 82 pairs and 82 mirror-image pairs.

2. Attach a dark green B (or B reverse) to the medium green A of each pair from Step 1. Make 82 units and 82 mirror-image units.

3. Pair each medium red A with a medium-light red A. Sew 82 of the pairs together along a straight edge with the medium red piece on top. Make 82 mirror-image pairs by sewing the remaining pairs together with the medium red piece on top. Make 82 pairs and 82 mirror-image pairs.

4. Attach a dark red B to the medium red A of 82 pairs from Step 3. Sew a dark red B Reverse to the medium red A of the 82 mirror-image pairs. Make 82 units and 82 mirror-image units.

5. Sew each green unit to a mirror-image red unit to make a top arc. Make 82. Sew each mirror-image green unit to a red unit to make a bottom arc. Make 82.

Make 82 top arcs.

Make 82 bottom arcs.

6. Lay the arcs right side down on an ironing surface. Press the seams toward the dark green side of the arcs.

7. Sew a very dark green C piece to the dark green B of each bottom arc. Sew a very dark red C piece to each dark red B of each bottom arc. Press the seams of the C pieces toward the middle of the arc.

8. Fold each cream D piece in half and crease to mark the center of the curve. With right sides facing, the arc on top, and the centers matching, sew a top arc to a cream D piece, starting and stopping at the marked dots and back-stitching at each end. Press the seam open. Make 82.

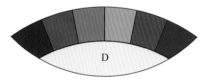

9. With right sides facing, the bottom arc on top, and the centers matching, sew a bottom arc to a unit created in the previous step. Press the seam open. Repeat to make 82 pieced melon units.

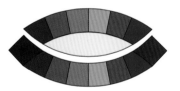

10. Fold each cream E piece in half horizontally, vertically, and diagonally, pressing after each fold to create appliqué placement lines.

11. For each appliquéd block center you will need 1 cream piece (E), 4 medium red flowers (F), 4 very dark green stems (G), 1 gold small flower (H), and 1 brown flower center (I). Following the appliqué placement diagram, use your preferred method to appliqué the Indiana Rose pieces to the cream E piece in alphabetical order.

Sometimes pieces added later will cover up the raw edges of pieces added earlier. *Note: You can reverse appliqué the brown I flower centers if you prefer.*

12. Following the Quilt Assembly Diagram on page 90, lay out the units created in Step 9 and the Indiana Rose E centers so that the colors are placed correctly, with very dark green C pieces touching and very dark red pieces touching.

13. With the cream E piece on top, pin an Indiana Rose center to a pieced melon unit created in Step 9. Match the centers, pin the marked dots of the E piece to the seam between the B and C pieces, and ease the E piece curve into place without stretching it. Sew only from dot to dot, backstitching at each end. Press toward the E piece.

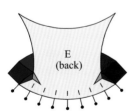

14. Attach 3 more pieced melon units in the same manner to make 1 complete ring, taking care to place the pieced melons so that the colors are correctly oriented. Press toward the center. Sew the very dark red and very dark green C piece seams from the dot to the edge. Press.

Make 1.

15. Make a three-quarter ring, following the piecing diagrams below and taking care to place the colors correctly. Repeat Steps 13–14, except sew only 3 pieced melons to the Indiana Rose center (E). Make 5 three-quarter rings and 5 mirror-image three-quarter rings.

Make 5.

Make 5.

16. Make a half-ring, following the piecing diagram below and taking care to place the colors correctly. Repeat Steps 13–14, except sew only 2 pieced melons to the Indiana Rose center (E). Sew the very dark red C piece seams from the dot to the edge. Press. Repeat to make 12 half-rings.

Make 12.

17. Make a mirror-image half-ring, following the piecing diagram below and taking care to place the colors correctly. Repeat Steps 13–14, except sew only 2 pieced melons to the Indiana Rose center (E). Sew the very dark green C piece seams from the dot to the edge. Press. Repeat to make 12 mirror-image half-rings.

Make 12.

18. Attach a very dark red C piece or a very dark green C piece to each three-quarter ring from Step 15 as shown below.

Make 3.

Make 3.

Make 2.

Make 2.

19. Sew 2 very dark green C pieces to a half-ring from Step 16 to make a lower right corner half-ring.

20. Sew a very dark red C piece or a very dark green C piece to 8 of the half-rings from Steps 16 and 17 as shown below.

Make 2.

Make 3.

Make 1.

Make 2.

Quilt Construction

1. Following the Quilt Assembly Diagram (page 90), lay out the full rings, three-quarter rings, and half-rings in the correct places.

2. With the Indiana Rose centers on top, right sides facing and centers matched, ease the curve of the cream E piece into place along the pieced melon and pin the adjacent rings together. Sew the rings into rows, stitching only from point to point on the cream E pieces. Press after each seam. Note: Do not sew the seams for the very dark red and very dark green C pieces. These will be sewn after the rows are joined.

3. Sew the rows together, stitching only from point to point on the cream E pieces. Press after each seam.

4. Now that the rows are joined, sew the last very dark red and very dark green seams. Each junction will have 2 seams. Keep the points of the cream E pieces free of the seams to reduce bulk. Press.

Sew seams 1 and 2 at each junction to complete the quilt top.

5. Layer the quilt top, batting, and backing. Baste. Quilt as desired.

6. From the very dark green fabric or another fabric of your choice, make approximately 450″ of double-fold bias binding. Pin the binding to the front of the quilt top, matching the raw edges. Ease the fullness around the curves, taking care not to stretch the binding as you go.

7. Begin sewing the binding to the quilt on a curve, not a point or a corner. Miter the very dark green and very dark red C points as you would the corners of a rectangular quilt. To bind the concave corners, when you reach a corner point, stop sewing with the needle in the down position; pivot the quilt top and resume sewing on the next ring.

8. When the binding is attached to the top of the quilt, fold the binding over to the back and hand stitch it down. To sew the curves, ease the binding into place without stretching it. For the points, miter as you would the corners of a rectangular quilt. For the inner corners, pin the binding in place at each corner and continue sewing the next ring. The binding will form a small tuck that you can sew closed later.

9. Attach a hanging sleeve, if desired. Sign and date your quilt on the back using permanent ink, embroidery, or a colorfast printed tag.

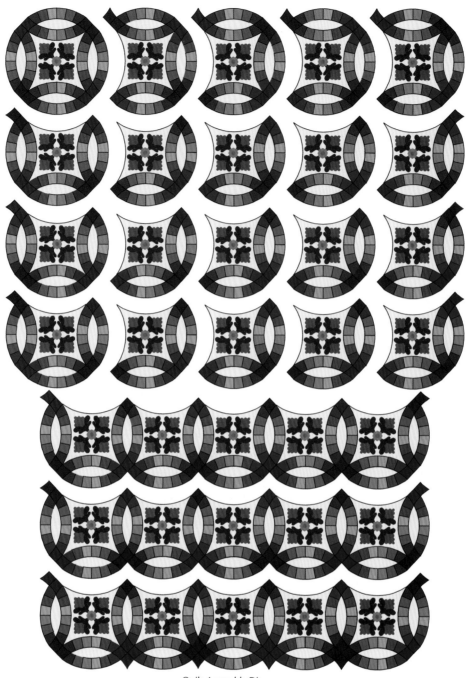

Quilt Assembly Diagram

QUILTMAKING BASICS
How to Finish Your Quilt

General Guidelines

Seam Allowances

A ¼" seam allowance is used for most projects. It's a good idea to do a test seam before you begin sewing to check that your ¼" is accurate. Accuracy is the key to successful piecing.

There is no need to backstitch unless specified. Seamlines will be crossed by another seam, which will anchor them.

Pressing

In general, press seams toward the darker fabric. Press lightly in an up-and-down motion. Avoid using a very hot iron or over-ironing, which can distort shapes and blocks. Be especially careful when pressing bias edges, as they stretch easily.

Borders

When border strips are cut on the crosswise grain, piece the strips together to achieve the needed lengths.

Butted Borders

In most cases the side borders are sewn on first. When you have finished the quilt top, measure it through the center vertically. This will be the length to cut the side borders. Place pins at the centers of all four sides of the quilt top, as well as in the center of each side border strip. Pin the side borders to the quilt top first, matching the center pins. Using a ¼" seam allowance, sew the borders to the quilt top and press toward the border.

Measure horizontally across the center of the quilt top including the side borders. This will be the length to cut the top and bottom borders. Repeat, pinning, sewing, and pressing.

Mitered Corner Borders

Measure the length of the quilt top and add two times the cut width of your border, plus 5". This is the length you need to cut or piece the side borders.

Place pins at the centers of both side borders and all four sides of the quilt top. From the center pin, measure in both directions and mark half of the measured length of the quilt top on both side borders. Pin, matching the centers and the marked length of the side border to the edges of the quilt top. Stitch the strips to the sides of the quilt top by starting ¼" in from the beginning edge of the quilt top, backstitching, and then continuing down the length of the side border. Stop stitching ¼" before the ending edge of the quilt top, at the seam allowance line, and backstitch. The excess length of the side borders will extend beyond each edge. Press the seams toward the borders.

Start stitching ¼" from the edge of the quilt top.

Stop stitching ¼" from the edge.

Determine the length needed for the top and bottom border the same way, measuring the width of the quilt top through the center including each side border. Add 2 times the cut width of your border plus 5" to this measurement. Cut or piece the top and bottom border strips to this length. From the center of each border strip, measure in both directions and mark half of the measured width of the quilt top. Again, pin, and start and stop stitching at the previous stitching lines, ¼" from the quilt edges and backstitch. The border strips extend beyond each end. Press the seams toward the borders.

To create the miter, lay the corner on the ironing board. Working with the quilt right side up, lay one border strip on top of the adjacent border.

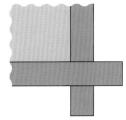

A border strip on top of the adjacent strip

With right sides up, fold the top border strip under itself so that it meets the edge of the adjacent border and forms a 45° angle. Pin the fold in place.

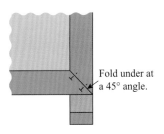

Fold under at a 45° angle.

Position a 90°-angle triangle or ruler over the corner to check that the corner is flat and square. When everything is in place, press the fold firmly.

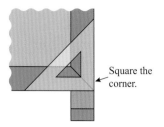

Square the corner.

Remove the pins. Fold the center section of the top diagonally from the corner, right sides together, and align the long edges of the border strips. On the wrong side, place pins near the pressed fold in the corner to secure the border strips.

Beginning at the inside corner at the border seamline, stitch, backstitch, and then stitch along the fold toward the outside point of the border corners, being careful not to allow any stretching to occur. Backstitch at the end. Trim the excess border fabric to a ¼" seam allowance. Press the seam open.

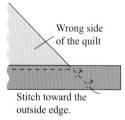

Wrong side of the quilt

Stitch toward the outside edge.

Stitch the mitered corner.

Backing

Plan on making the backing a minimum of 8" longer and wider than the quilt top. Piece, if necessary. Trim the selvages before you piece to the desired size.

To economize, piece the back from any leftover quilting fabrics or blocks in your collection.

Batting

The type of batting to use is a personal decision; consult your local quilt shop. Cut the batting approximately 8" longer and wider than your quilt top. Note that your batting choice will affect how much quilting is necessary for the quilt. Check the manufacturer's instructions to see how far apart the quilting lines can be.

Layering

Spread the backing wrong side up and tape the edges down with masking tape. (If you are working on carpet you can use T-pins to secure the backing to the carpet.) Center the batting on top, smoothing out any folds. Place the quilt top right side up on top of the batting and backing, making sure it is centered.

Basting

Basting keeps the quilt "sandwich" layers from shifting while you are quilting.

If you plan to machine quilt, pin baste the quilt layers together with safety pins placed a minimum of 3"–4" apart. Begin basting in the center and move toward the edges first in vertical, then horizontal, rows. Try not to pin directly on the intended quilting lines.

If you plan to hand quilt, baste the layers together with thread using a long needle and light-colored thread. Knot one end of the thread. Using stitches approximately the length of the needle, begin in the center and move out toward the edges in vertical and horizontal rows approximately 4" apart. Add 2 diagonal rows of basting.

Quilting

Quilting, whether by hand or machine, enhances the pieced or appliquéd design of the quilt. You may choose to quilt in-the-ditch, echo the pieced or appliqué motifs, use patterns from quilting design books and stencils, or do your own free-motion quilting. Remember to check your batting manufacturer's recommendations for how close the quilting lines must be.

Binding

Trim excess batting and backing from the quilt even with the edges of the quilt top.

Double-Fold Straight-Grain Binding

If you want a ¼" finished binding, cut the binding strips 2" wide and piece them together with diagonal seams to make a continuous binding strip. Trim the seam allowance to ¼". Press the seams open.

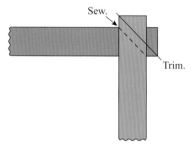

Sew.

Trim.

Sew from corner to corner.

Completed diagonal seam

Press the entire strip in half lengthwise with wrong sides together. With raw edges even, pin the binding to the front edge of the quilt a few inches away from the corner, and leave the first few inches of the binding unattached. Start sewing, using a ¼" seam allowance.

Stop ¼" away from the first corner (see Step 1) and backstitch one stitch. Lift the presser foot and needle. Rotate the quilt one-quarter turn. Fold the binding at a right angle so it extends straight above the quilt and the fold forms a 45° angle in the corner (see Step 2). Then bring the binding strip down even with the edge of the quilt (see Step 3). Begin sewing at the folded edge. Repeat in the same manner at all corners.

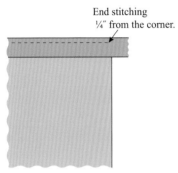

Step 1. Stitch to 1/4" from the corner.

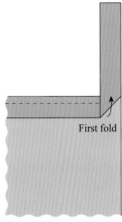

Step 2. First fold for the miter

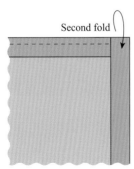

Step 3. Second fold alignment

Continue stitching until you are back near the beginning of the binding strip. See Finishing the Binding Ends for tips on finishing and hiding the raw edges of the ends of the binding.

Continuous Bias Binding

A continuous bias involves using a square sliced in half diagonally and then sewing the triangles together so that you continuously cut marked strips to make continuous bias binding. The same instructions can be used to cut bias for piping. Cut the fabric for the bias binding or piping so it is a square. For example, if yardage is ½ yard, cut an 18" × 18" square. Cut the square in half diagonally, creating two triangles.

Sew these triangles together as shown, using a ¼" seam allowance. Press the seam open.

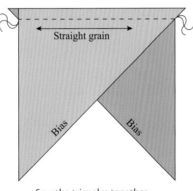

Sew the triangles together.

Using a ruler, mark the parallelogram created by the 2 triangles with lines spaced the width you need to cut your bias. Cut about 5" along the first line.

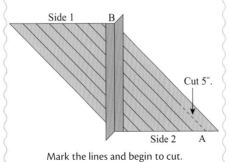

Mark the lines and begin to cut.

Join side 1 and side 2 to form a tube. The raw edge at line A will align with the raw edge at B. This will allow the first line to be offset by one strip width. Pin the raw edges right sides together, making sure that the lines match. Sew with a ¼" seam allowance. Press the seam open. Cut along the drawn lines, creating one continuous strip.

Press the entire strip in half lengthwise with wrong sides together. Place the binding on the quilt as described in Double-Fold Straight-Grain Binding (above).

See Finishing the Binding Ends for tips on finishing and hiding the raw edges of the ends of the binding.

Finishing the Binding Ends
METHOD 1

After stitching around the quilt, fold under the beginning tail of the binding strip ¼" so that the raw edge will be inside the binding after it is turned to the back side of the quilt. Place the end tail of the binding strip over the beginning folded end. Continue to attach the binding and stitch slightly beyond the starting stitches. Trim the excess binding. Fold the binding over the raw edges to the quilt back and hand stitch, mitering the corners.

METHOD 2

See our blog entry at ctpubblog.com; search for "invisible seam;" then scroll down to "Quilting Tips: Completing a Binding with an Invisible Seam."

Fold the ending tail of the binding back on itself where it meets the beginning binding tail. From the fold, measure and mark the cut width of your binding strip. Cut the ending binding tail to this measurement. For example, if your binding is cut 2⅛" wide, measure from the fold on the ending tail of the binding 2⅛" and cut the binding tail to this length.

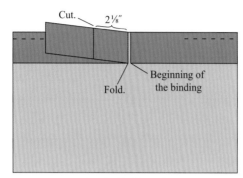

Cut the binding tail.

Open both tails. Place one tail on top of the other tail at right angles, right sides together. Mark a diagonal line from corner to corner and stitch on the line. Check that you've done it correctly and that the binding fits the quilt; then trim the seam allowance to ¼". Press open.

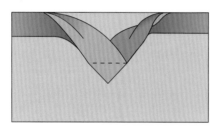

Stitch the ends of the binding diagonally.

Refold the binding and stitch this binding section in place on the quilt. Fold the binding over the raw edges to the quilt back and hand stitch.

Half-Square Triangles

Refer to the project instructions for the size of the squares.

1. With right sides together, pair 2 squares. Lightly draw a diagonal line from one corner to the opposite corner on the wrong side of a square.

Draw a line.

2. Sew a scant ¼" seam on each side of the line.

Sew.

3. Cut on the drawn line.

4. Press, and trim off the dog-ears.

About the Author

Jennifer Chiaverini is the author of the *New York Times* bestselling Elm Creek Quilts series, which currently includes eighteen titles and more than 1.5 million copies sold. She is also the author of five collections of quilt projects inspired by the novels and designs the Elm Creek Quilts fabric lines for Red Rooster Fabrics. A graduate of the University of Notre Dame and the University of Chicago, she lives in Madison, Wisconsin, with her husband and two sons.

Author photograph by Steven Garfinkel

Also by Jennifer Chiaverini:

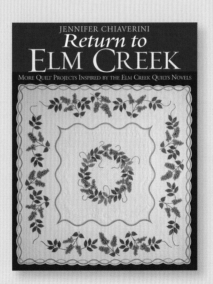

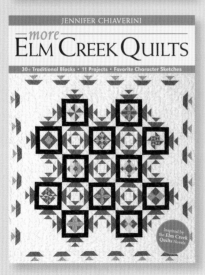

Great Titles *from* C&T PUBLISHING & STASH BOOKS

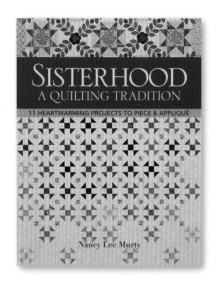

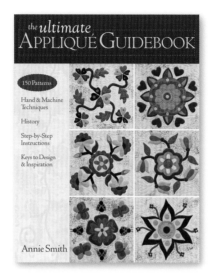

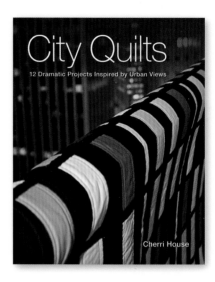

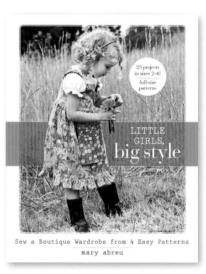

Available at your local retailer or **www.ctpub.com** *or* **800-284-1114**

For a list of other fine books from C&T Publishing, visit our website to view our catalog online.

C&T PUBLISHING, INC.
P.O. Box 1456
Lafayette, CA 94549
800-284-1114

Email: ctinfo@ctpub.com
Website: www.ctpub.com

C&T Publishing's professional photography services are now available to the public. Visit us at www.ctmediaservices.com.

Tips and Techniques can be found at www.ctpub.com > Consumer

For quilting supplies:

COTTON PATCH
1025 Brown Ave.
Lafayette, CA 94549
Store: 925-284-1177
Mail order: 925-283-7883

Email: CottonPa@aol.com
Website: www.quiltusa.com

Note: Fabrics used in the quilts shown may not be currently available, as fabric manufacturers keep most fabrics in print for only a short time.